0 4 MAR 2010	2 4 OCT 2016	
0 1 APR 2010	1 4 JUL 2017	
	3 0 JAN 2018	
1 1 SEP 2010		
2 5 JAN 2011		
14 FEB ''	1 6 FEB 2018	
2 3 NOV 2012	1 4 JUL 2018	
1 4 JUN 2014	1 9 NOV 2018	

This book should be returned/renewed by
the latest date shown above. Overdue items
incur charges which prevent self-service
renewals. Please contact the library.

Wandsworth Libraries
24 hour Renewal Hotline
01527 852
www.wandsworth.gov.uk Wandsworth

L.749A (rev.11.2004)

www.wandsworth.gov.uk Wandsworth

L.749A (rev.11.2004)

D1341188

WALKING LONDON'S
DOCKS, RIVERS & CANALS

GILLY CAMERON-COOPER

NEW
HOLLAND

501338236

First published in 2005 by
New Holland Publishers (UK) Ltd
London • Cape Town • Sydney • Auckland

www.newhollandpublishers.com

Garfield House
86–88 Edgware Road
London W2 2EA
United Kingdom

80 McKenzie Street
Cape Town 8001
South Africa

14 Aquatic Drive
Frenchs Forest, NSW 2086
Australia

218 Lake Road
Northcote, Auckland
New Zealand

ISBN 1 84330 902 5

Publishing Manager: Jo Hemmings
Senior Editor: Kate Michell
Copy Editor: Charlotte Rundall
Assistant Editor: Rose Hudson
Cartographer: William Smuts
Designer: Gülen Shevki-Taylor
Indexer: Dorothy Frame
Production: Joan Woodroffe

Reproduction by Pica Colour Separation Overseas (Pte) Ltd, Singapore
Printed and bound in Singapore by Kyodo Printing Co (Singapore) Pte Ltd

CONTENTS

INTRODUCTION

I thought I knew London well; I have cycled from many a suburb to the centre, clawed my way around it by car and written many a city walk. Nevertheless, my ideal of exploring places on foot has generally been among the sculpted mountains, luscious valleys and dazzling shores of the Greek island where I run walking holidays with my husband. Nothing could be more dramatically different than the industrial and urban landscapes of London's docklands and waterways. A poor alternative, you might think, but no, London's waterways offer exciting, rewarding and ever-changing territory, rich in history, discovery and even opportunities for some wildlife watching. You deepen your knowledge and understanding of one of the world's greatest capital cities, reaching parts you never knew existed – and most of these paths are passable for walking at any time of the year. I hope that exploring the docks, rivers and canals will reveal for you, as it did for me, new perspectives, less familiar scenes and an insight into London's industrial history.

Breathing Space
Looking at London from the perspective of its waterways presents a different world, another level of existence away from the familiar sprawl of streets and arterial roads, shops, houses and offices. Ribbons of almost-rural green wind through unseen industrial and urban wastelands, concealed from view by graceful willows and poplars. Here, sheltered from the roar of traffic and the pace of city life, kingfishers dart, herons stand and wild flowers flourish. You may find yourself strolling beside a green-fringed canal, brown carp loitering just beneath the water's surface and gaily painted narrowboats sliding by, then catch the name of a familiar road on a bridge and marvel at the times you used that road in complete ignorance of the hidden world that lay beneath. In unexpected places, such as Woolwich, Bermondsey or London's old East End, you will discover a watery cut or basin lined with plane trees and pebbled paths, and occasional gems of modern landscaping that evoke the byways of Amsterdam.

Peeling Back the Past
London's docks, rivers and canals offer far more than welcome breathing space in a capital city. They are soaked in layers of history. The very life and development of London as a port, commercial centre and cultural capital evolved and revolved around its location on the River Thames, and

the city's rises and falls in fortune are reflected in the stories its waterways have to tell.

Sometimes, you may feel that the docks and canals of today, bereft of the jobs for which they were created, are sterile and lifeless compared with, for example, 150 years ago, when they were vital links in the global trade of a thriving industrial nation. However, anyone walking along a waterway of that time would probably have been overwhelmed by the stench and detritus of industrial and urban pollution. Today, thanks to the efforts of organizations such as British Waterways, enlightened local councils and conservation groups, pedestrians not only have unprecedented access to waterside paths, but can see aquatic plants and fish in the relatively clean water and breathe relatively fresh air.

It is their history, however, that makes these waterways particularly interesting to walk along, and the more you learn, the more you are able to look at a building or a scene and peel back the layers of its past. As you stand on the embankment of the River Thames at Blackfriars or Bermondsey you can imagine the broad tidal river that greeted Roman invaders in the 1st century AD: the river was sluggish between its silted shores and flanked by wastes of low-lying marshland dotted with tribal settlements, with the dense woodland of the Great Middlesex Forest beyond. You can mentally substitute the high-rises of new Docklands for Georgian docks packed with a bristling forest of masts, and the suburbs of Brentford and Wembley for the market gardens, which, at the beginning of the 19th century, dominated the countryside within 5–10 miles (8–16km) of the city, providing fruit, vegetables, meat and dairy products for the ever-growing population.

Exploring the city's waterways is to reach the heart of London's history. Stone Age people may have settled on the hillocks we now know as Ludgate (see page 157, *Bridging the Thames* walk) and Cornhill, protected by the Thames to the south and marshlands to the north and well-watered by springs and streams such as the long-lost Walbrook and Fleet rivers. Soon after the Romans had established their control of Britain in the 1st century AD, Londinium, as they were to call the new settlement, became the obvious choice for a commercial and administrative centre. Gravel that had washed down to the mudflats by floods had formed shallows, which could be forded or bridged, and beaches, which provided firm ground for landing. The river became an increasingly busy trading route, carrying supplies to and from the rest of the Roman Empire, and the port of Londinium grew in importance.

Ships could sail up the Thames estuary and ride the high tide along the river, spreading the influence of invaders, such as the Vikings and French, on Britain's lifestyle and language far inland. These invaders also introduced exotic products and new trade, establishing London as the port and commercial centre that would eventually dominate the world. You will pass inlets where the Romans traded in wine and corn and the shores where our Saxon ancestors loaded bales of woven cloth to be shipped to the weavers of the Low Countries. You will gaze over reaches of the Thames from which adventurers set forth to find new trade routes in the age of exploration and walk along waterways that were once the pulsing arteries of communication in Britain. The piers, wharves, bridges and waterside buildings of the distant past have long crumbled or been covered by layers of silt and buildings. But the foundations of modern industrial England are still very much in evidence along the routes covered by this book.

Proximity to the sea meant that the lower reaches of the Thames and Lea rivers were tidal, a force that was harnessed to power tidal mills. The energy of tributaries flowing into the Thames, such as the Wandle and the Ravensbourne rivers, was also utilized: to power mills for grinding corn, gunpowder or snuff, or to drive machines that whittled water conduits from tree trunks or sharpened metal into sewing needles. The combination of its local resources, proximity to northern Europe, and Thames-side location put London ahead of rival ports, such as Bristol and Portsmouth, making it Britain's capital and principal port, the focal point of both global and national trade and communications. The engineering feats of the Georgians and Victorians – which included an ambitious network of canals, massive dock-building programmes, bridges, viaducts, locks and steam engines – put Britain at the forefront of the modern industrial world, in which London played a pivotal role.

Exploring London's waterways provides an evocative insight into the extraordinary changes and achievements of the Industrial Revolution particularly, but also into Britain's pioneering marine technology, impressive achievements in trading and exploration, and social history through the ages. Because of their active contribution to the life of London – and Britain – the landscapes bordering the waterways have been prone to extraordinary upheavals and facelifts, of changing trades and industries, fortunes and populations throughout history.

London's Lost Rivers

There were victims of London's success story. Many of the rivers and millstreams that once provided clear spring water – at Clerkenwell, for example – were lost. As the city grew, marshland was drained and rivers were redirected and tamed by dams and sluices, banished to underground conduits and relegated to carrying sewage. Their courses were bricked over and, through the centuries, became hidden beneath successive layers of buildings, rubbish and road and rail routes. You may have been able to enjoy their bucolic attractions in the 11th century, but now the lost rivers are only remembered in the names of streets and suburbs, such as Holborn (meaning stream in the hollow), Fleet Street, Marshgate, Stratford and Knightsbridge, which is on the course of the Westbourne.

This book investigates the surviving rivers, such as the Wandle, the Brent and the Lea, which still offer waterside walks of great interest and some rural relief in an urban area. It is a different, but challenging experience to trace, via the pavements of central London, the courses of the lost rivers. A name plate on the Thames Path near Cannon Street Station recalls the one-time emergence of the Walbrook there (though the historian John Stow records that the small river was covered with buildings as long ago as 1598). The Fleet, once one of the largest of the Thames tributaries, degenerated into a brook that was frequently choked with rubbish, industrial effluent, raw sewage and dead animals. The Fleet was made into a canal after the Great Fire of London and then bricked over. Its present-day role is as a storm sewer emptying into the Thames at Blackfriars Bridge. The Serpentine lake in Hyde Park lies in the valley once fed by the Westbourne: the river itself is transported in underground pipes, which can be seen at Sloane Square Underground Station and emptying into the Thames at Chelsea. Pipes carrying the waters of the Tyburn pass through Victoria and Baker Street underground stations.

Exploring the Waterways

This book aims to give a sense of the history that shaped and was shaped by the waterways which you can still see, whether they be natural or manmade. I skim over many 'sights' en route – along the Thames especially – that owe little to waterside history and are well covered in more general walking books.

Most of the Thames-side and canal-side routes are all-weather gravel or better, but some of the riverside walks can be extremely muddy and comfortable Wellington boots are perhaps the most appropriate footwear. Some words of warning: a few routes go through rundown and remote areas, where it is safer to walk with a friend or a dog; direction signs on the trails are not always reliable as it is a popular sport in some localities to rotate the signs upon their posts so that they point in any direction but the correct one; other direction signs – and sadly this also applies to many of the local wildlife or history information boards – are obscured by graffiti; and signposting and trail directions found on websites tend to lack in detail and consistency.

The landscape is still changing: even in the course of writing this book a hotel was demolished, a statue was taken away for cleaning and a new footbridge and a section of a riverside path opened. Initiatives to improve the environment and urban redevelopment schemes to support London's bid to host the 2012 Olympic Games may well have a major impact on the urban landscapes you are walking through. I hope that you find the directions in this book clear, but please write to the publisher if you have difficulties and we will make every attempt to make the necessary corrections when the book is reprinted.

Finally, I hope that using this book will give you as much pleasure as I had from researching and writing it. Our walking business on an idyllic Greek island is now happily complemented by discovering London's docks, rivers and canals!

Gilly Cameron-Cooper, www.walkingplus.co.uk

KEY TO MAPS

Each of the walks is accompanied by a map in which the route is shown in blue. Places of interest along the walk, such as historic buildings and open spaces, are clearly identified, as are all underground and railway stations along the routes.

The following is a key to the symbols used on the maps:

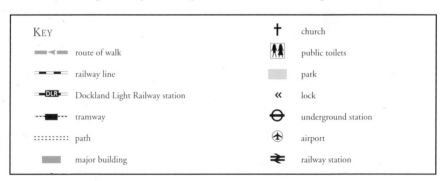

KEY		
route of walk	†	church
railway line	🏃🏃	public toilets
Dockland Light Railway station		park
tramway	«	lock
path	⊖	underground station
major building	✈	airport
	⇌	railway station

Opposite: Elegant Hammersmith Bridge (see pages 159–67, Sporting Thames walk) is an important landmark in the University Boat Race. When it opened in 1827 it became the first suspension bridge across the River Thames.

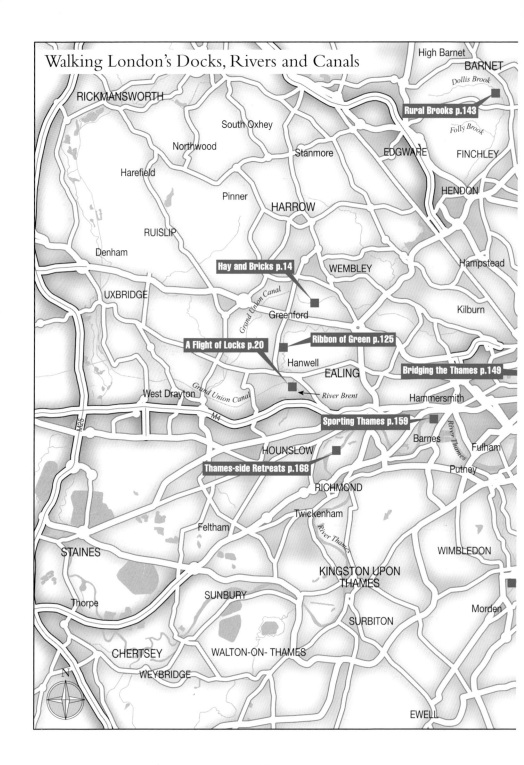

Walking London's Docks, Rivers and Canals

High Barnet

BARNET

Dollis Brook

RICKMANSWORTH

Rural Brooks p.143

Folly Brook

South Oxhey

Northwood

Stanmore

EDGWARE   **FINCHLEY**

Harefield

HENDON

Pinner

HARROW

RUISLIP

Denham

WEMBLEY

Hampstead

UXBRIDGE

Hay and Bricks p.14

Grand Union Canal

Greenford

Kilburn

A Flight of Locks p.20

Ribbon of Green p.125

Hanwell

EALING

Bridging the Thames p.149

Grand Union Canal

West Drayton

← *River Brent*

Hammersmith

M25

M4

Sporting Thames p.159

River Thames

HOUNSLOW

Barnes

Fulham

Thames-side Retreats p.168

Putney

RICHMOND

Twickenham

River Thames

Feltham

STAINES

WIMBLEDON

KINGSTON UPON THAMES

Thorpe

SUNBURY

Morden

SURBITON

CHERTSEY

WALTON-ON- THAMES

WEYBRIDGE

N

EWELL

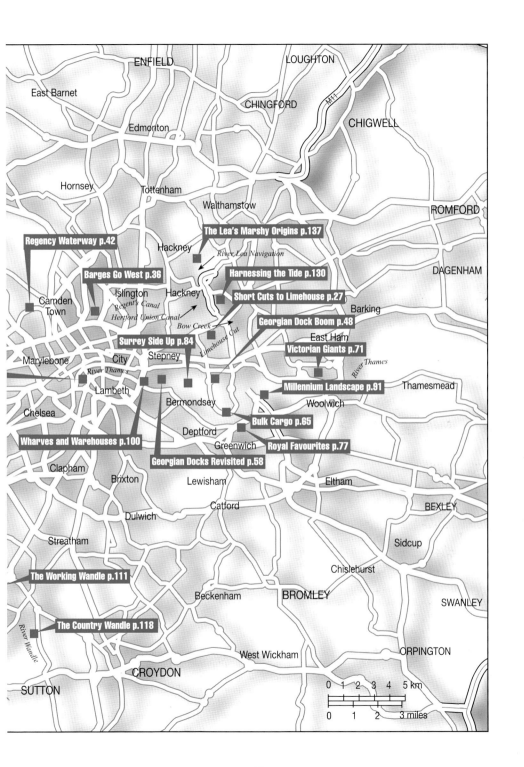

ENFIELD

LOUGHTON

East Barnet

CHINGFORD

CHIGWELL

M11

Edmonton

Hornsey

Tottenham

ROMFORD

Walthamstow

The Lea's Marshy Origins p.137

DAGENHAM

Regency Waterway p.42

Hackney

River Lea Navigation

Barges Go West p.36

Harnessing the Tide p.130

Islington

Hackney

Short Cuts to Limehouse p.27

Camden
Town

Regent's Canal

Barking

Hertford Union Canal

Bow Creek

Georgian Dock Boom p.48

Surrey Side Up p.84

Limehouse Cut

East Ham

Victorian Giants p.71

Marylebone

City

Stepney

River Thames

River Thames

Thamesmead

Lambeth

Millennium Landscape p.91

Chelsea

Bermondsey

Woolwich

Bulk Cargo p.65

Deptford

Wharves and Warehouses p.100

Greenwich

Royal Favourites p.77

Clapham

Georgian Docks Revisited p.58

Brixton

Lewisham

Eltham

Dulwich

Catford

BEXLEY

Streatham

Sidcup

The Working Wandle p.111

Chislehurst

Beckenham

BROMLEY

SWANLEY

The Country Wandle p.118

River Wandle

ORPINGTON

West Wickham

CROYDON

0 1 2 3 4 5 km

SUTTON

0   1   2   3 miles

HAY AND BRICKS: GRAND UNION CANAL, HORSENDEN HILL AREA

Summary: We explore the Paddington Arm of the Grand Junction (later Grand Union) Canal along its most rural and leafy stretch, learning on the way about narrowboats and their cargoes. To the west, the Paddington Arm continues rather more grubbily through densely populated Greenford and Southall to Bull's Bridge junction, where it joins the main canal, but our route takes us up Horsenden Hill, with its sensational views over the London basin, so that we can reflect on the ages of this landscape from 5000 BC to the present day.

Start:	Greenford Underground and Railway Station
Finish:	Alperton Underground Station
Distance:	4.5 miles (7.5km)
Refreshments:	Pleasure Boat pub, Alperton

Turn right from Greenford Station and walk along Rockware Avenue as far as the traffic lights. Cross the road obliquely left to the cycle path (signed to Perivale) and turn left along it. In this pleasantly conserved meadowland you can begin to imagine how so much of the area bordering this part of the canal looked when, from the 16th century onwards, it was a major supplier of fodder to London's road and canal horses. Then, Green*ford* was a rural parish that had grown up around an ancient river crossing, teaming up with other river crossings at Brentford near the Thames and Middle Ford in between the two, near Hanwell.

In the 19th century, Greenford was the local centre of commerce, and by the middle of the century, around 1,000 tons of hay were taken by canal to London each year. Greenford was consumed by suburbia, factories and industrial estates, losing its last shreds of individuality when three major roads were cut through it and the land between was developed in the 1920s and 1930s. The initial trigger for north-west London's development, however, was the 13.5-mile (22.5-km) Paddington Arm of the Grand Junction (later the Grand Union) Canal, which we are just about to join.

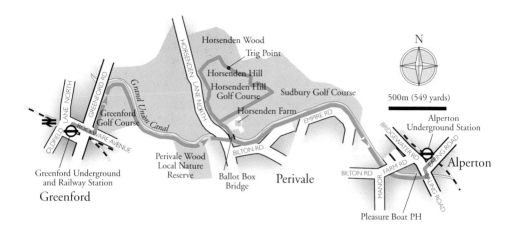

As you follow the cycle path round to the right, the rise of Horsenden Hill provides a backdrop to the meadowland, which, in the summer months, is full of wild flowers, such as mauve and white vetches, and great willowherb. Willows mark the course of a stream and then you will see a wooden footbridge, which announces your approach to the canal. Turn left just before the bridge to turn right beneath it and walk along the towpath.

A Slice of History

The course of the Paddington Arm of the canal is like a core sample of history, piercing the surrounding suburbia and arterial roads. It recalls an age of waterside hay fields, market gardens and a crowded waterway. The 'arm' was completed in the early 19th century, and was busy from the start. It had taken just six years to build, aided by the fact that its course was so level that no locks were needed. The new canal extension provided a cheap, efficient and direct commercial route all the way from Birmingham and the Midlands to the centre of London. Until the Paddington Arm was built, the Grand Junction Canal had terminated much further upstream on the Thames, at Brentford. Barges and narrowboats from Paddington Basin in central London could now continue west and south to join the main Grand Union Canal at Bull's Bridge, then take a right turn to central England. Here, they were joined by boats on their way to or from the Thames at Brentford (see pages 20–26, *Flight of Locks* walk) via the canalized River Brent. The last key commercial link was made when the Regent's Canal was completed in 1820; this extended the Paddington Arm route east to the Thames at Limehouse and the London docklands. When the Grand Junction Canal Company merged with the companies that ran the Regent's and Warwick canals in 1929, the waterway came under the Grand Union Canal umbrella, and so gained its present name.

The canal here is broad, peaceful and richly bordered with green. The occasional narrowboat chugs peacefully into sight – in contrast to the scene about 150 years ago, when a steady stream of narrowboats transported hay and bricks, which were made in works set up beside the canal to take advantage of the local clay, easy transport and a ready supply of coal transported along the canal. Boats on the return journey to Greenford brought 'mack', which was a mixture of domestic waste and offal, to fertilize the local hay fields and market gardens. Although aggregates, waste and materials for recycling are carried along the canal today, the boats you see are more likely to be for leisure, either purpose-built or with the cargo area converted into living space.

On the Paddington Arm, narrowboats – so named for their slender dimensions (traditionally 7 feet (just over 2m) wide and about 70 feet (20m) long) – would have dominated the scene, in contrast to the broader barges of the Thames waterways. At the beginning of the Canal Age, the boats were simply cargo carriers operated by teams of men and had no living space at all. Then, with the coming of the railways, boatmen moved on board with their families, combining work, home and family life to cut costs and keep freight prices competitive. Living space was minimal: kitchen, bedroom and living room were crammed into an area just 10 feet x 7 feet (3m x 2m). Extra cargo space might be provided by a 'butty', an engineless narrowboat that was towed by the lead boat.

Towpath and canal border the fenced-in green area of Perivale Wood Local Nature Reserve on the right, a 27-acre (11-hectare) remnant of the once-mighty, post-glacial Great Middlesex Forest, which was gradually slashed and burned to make way for cultivation and then urban development. Today, it is a Site of Special Scientific Interest (SSSI), but open to the public on just one day a year, at bluebell time in May.

Continue until you reach a small white bridge, about 20 minutes after leaving Greenford Station. This is Ballot Box Bridge, which was built in 1909. Turn right just after the bridge and turn back on yourself to go over it. A farm has been recorded on the site of Horsenden Visitors' Centre on your right since the 16th century. The centre's opening has been delayed by subsidence due to water run-off from Horsenden Hill, but a cafeteria is planned. Go past the entrance to the centre and along the road for a few yards and then turn right. Take the path to the right of the tarmac path, up some steps to wild grassland. Here, in late summer, are bright splashes of yellow from stands of tall goldenrod, which was once cut and sold as a wound-healing herb. However, the bottom fell out of the goldenrod market because the plant was so common. The soft pink-purple blooms of great willowherb, commonly known as codlins-and-cream, add contrast to the colour palette. From June to September, look out for the shrubby dyer's greenweed, with its bright yellow flowers; it is a broomlike member of the pea family from which a yellow pigment was extracted that could be blended with blue woad to make a rich green.

Horsenden Hill

Ignore all minor turnings to the left. When the route levels out, just before rejoining the tarmac path and a metalled road to the car park, turn right up a cobbled track. This takes you to the summit of Horsenden Hill. It's only 276 feet (85m) above sea level, but is a fine vantage point from which you can imagine the layers of landscape history beneath the spread of London and suburbia towards Windsor Castle in the west and the Post Office Tower, the London Eye and the City to the east.

The post-glacial forests of oak and shrubby woodland made way for cultivated land and small settlements; then came the vast hay fields and market gardens of the 18th and 19th centuries to feed the ravening London markets. Although their wooden hafts have long since rotted, flint arrowheads from some 7,000 years ago have been found on Horsenden Hill, evidence that the site was on the seasonal hunting and gathering circuit of nomadic Stone Age tribes. Later people took advantage of the hill's defensive position when they began to clear land, cultivate crops for food, rear and keep animals and generally settle down, building a cluster of small round houses. Fragments of their pottery from around 2,500 years ago have been found, and the hill's name – from the Saxon *Horsa's Dun*, meaning 'horse's down' – is thought to refer to these ancient people's reputation as skilled horsemen, though some say that Horsa may have been a Saxon chief.

The forest clearance continued, and more and more of the hill was turned into fields until, by the 14th century, it was producing crops of wheat, barley, corn and rye. Hay fields dominated the hill from the 16th to the 19th century, by which time the local canal transport was playing a key role. Then, in the First World War (1914–18), the hill's prime defensive position came into play when an anti-aircraft gun was positioned on the summit to target German airships. Soon after the war ended, the first wave of factory building began and major roads were constructed in the 1930s. During the Second World War (1939–45), the hill had a searchlight station on the alert for attacks on local factories, which had been turned over to armaments manufacture. Once again the surrounding fields were planted with crops, this time as part of the war effort.

Cross the summit diagonally via the trig point in the direction of the distant Post Office Tower. Wild grassland merges into golf course and your route is, for a while, dictated by the golf course's features. At the seventh tee, take the main path sharp right. Pass the sixth tee and return again to a slice of English countryside in the form of a wood-lined grassy path. At the bottom, turn right to return to the tarmac path at Ballot Box Bridge. Cross the bridge and return to the towpath to go right towards Alperton. On the right are suburban gardens. Along the towpath you might find a healthy clump of the once-common horseradish plant, the roots of which are the main ingredient of the pungent sauce that complements roast beef.

Burgeoning Industry

There's a long stretch now that is attractive enough as you look across to Horsenden Hill, but it can be muddy in winter. It is apt that the last bridge you pass under on this walk is of red brick, for bricks and other building materials, such as sand and gravel, were the most important cargoes along the Paddington Arm in the mid-19th century. There were kilns upstream at West Drayton, Yiewsley and Hayes, and the opening of the canal transformed the farming village of Alperton, which in 1805 consisted of just 21 houses and 14 farms. Soon, shipments of coal (canal transport cut the price of coal by half), hay and construction materials were being handled here and brick- and tile-making industries were established nearby. A pleasure-boat service ferried Londoners on a day trip to the Pleasure Boat pub, which overlooks the opposite bank of the canal, and this became a favourite resort of anglers. All too soon, however, Alperton became the most industrialized village in Wembley, and the odours of pigswill and dung from the remaining farms mingled with industrial smoke and a local sewage farm.

As you pass under the red-brick bridge, towards a blue high-rise block ahead, look down to the canal bank for the rusting remains of a stop gate mechanism, which is now partly hidden by vegetation. The stop gate, with its downstream partner, was a guard against the canal water bursting its banks in the event of a bomb strike. If this were to happen, the gates could be lowered to stop the flow of water and reduce flooding downstream. Just before the next (concrete) bridge, peel off to the right and up the steps; head left across the bridge and take the first right, Ealing Road, to Alperton Underground Station.

Opposite: The Grand Union Canal towpath winds beneath Horsenden Hill, which is a haven of meadows and broadleaved woodland hidden among the suburbs and arterial roads of north-west London.

A FLIGHT OF LOCKS: GRAND UNION CANAL, BRENTFORD–HANWELL

Summary: Brentford is the gateway to the Thames from the inland waterways of England, once an important meeting point of road, rail, canal and river. It was a fortified ford during the Roman occupation (AD 43–84) and after the 18th century it was once a market garden for London. If you're used to seeing the area from the A4 road, this is a walk that takes you through surprising hidden gems in suburbia, past muddy banks and herons, covered wharves and – if you go in late summer or early autumn – lots of blackberries to where you can see a flight of locks in action at Hanwell.

Start:	Kew Bridge Railway Station
Finish:	Hanwell Railway Station
Distance:	6 miles (10km)
Refreshments:	Waterman's Arts Centre; The Fox Stop pub at Hanwell Locks

Turn right out of Kew Bridge Station and go along Kew Bridge Road for a couple of hundred yards to the tall brick tower on the right. This is the Kew Bridge Steam Museum, formerly the Grand Junction Water Works Company. From 1838 until 1944, water was pumped from the Thames by massive steam engines housed in this building, then cleaned and treated before being pumped onward to households and factories from Sunbury to Kensington.

Nature Trail

From the museum, turn left back towards Kew Bridge, cross the road at the traffic lights, and go down the slip road on the right-hand side of the bridge. Continue down to the River Thames and turn right, signed The Hollows. Follow this leafy path lined with buddleia, balsam, willow and the miniature garden plots of moored house-boats. At a cobbled circle with a semicircular iron bench, turn right up some steps to the main road. Turn left, and after only a few yards, past Victoria Steps car park, turn left again to enter Waterside Park. The path is high above a muddy backwater of the

Thames that seeps behind the islands of Brentford Ait and Lots Ait and is littered with neglected vessels, some supporting spontaneous wildflife gardens. The islands have trees thick and lush in high summer. Beyond the church tower to the right, the path meets the red-brick building of the Waterman's Arts Centre; cut up right to the terrace for a drink or continue along the path to the end of the building, turn right down some steps at the back, and right into the car park. Turn left out of the car park, right up the stepped path to the main road and cross it into Ealing Road. Take the first left into Albany Road, then second right (Brook Road South) and first left into Grosvenor Road. At the end, go straight across the recreation ground along an avenue of lime trees and past a Victorian fountain into St Paul's Road. Go straight ahead, past the little Victorian school on the left with its separate entrances for boys and girls, to cross the wide road called Half Acre, then turn right. After a few yards, turn left into an elegant tree-lined residential avenue called The Butts: 'The Butts Estate' is engraved into a stone plaque on the wall at the entrance.

Victorian residential architecture precedes a delightful enclave of Georgian and Queen Anne houses, some dating back to the 1680s. They recall a time when Brentford was a grand place to live, close enough to London but a town of some standing in its own right. In Victorian times, traffic into London increased, as more and more produce was taken from the surrounding farms and market gardens along the long-established main route over the River Brent. Brentford became notorious for the mud churned up on its overused roads, and for its concentration of breweries and other factories.

The Grand Junction

Cross the square (a former marketplace) diagonally to the far left corner before turning left into a road called Market Place. Continue straight ahead, passing Brentford Magistrates Court on the right, and turn right at the main road. In a couple of minutes you cross the bridge over the River Brent and turn right on the far side of the bridge to Brentford Lock, the first indication that the river is not in its natural state. The Brent was not navigable until 1794, when it was tamed and straightened into an extension of the Grand Junction Canal, the final link in a through-route between the Midlands and the River Thames. The Grand Junction's engineer was William Jessop. His brief was to create a waterway that would slice 60 miles (100km) off the trade route between London and Birmingham. He went further than this, providing a solution to the usual bottlenecks at locks by making his locks double width at 14 feet (over 4m), so that two 7-foot-wide (2-m) narrowboats could squeeze through simultaneously. It also made the locks accessible to the wider 70-ton barges that worked the downstream waterways and the Thames.

At Brentford Lock, barges and their freight were checked in and their operators charged a toll based on type of boat and weight of cargo. Later, in 1859, the Great Western Railway, carrying freight from Bristol and from western and southern England, was extended to Brentford, and the surrounding area – especially between the lock and the Thames (see pages 168–75, *Thames-side Retreats* walk) – became densely packed with warehouses, workshops, freight sheds and a railway marshalling yard. All gradually fell into disuse in the mid-20th century, but since the 1970s the area has been redeveloped to provide desirable waterside housing.

Shadowing the M4

Soon the path goes interestingly under cover beneath overhanging warehouses. This was the Brentford Depot, a freight terminal at which barges and cargo carriers (called lighters) from the downstream Thames and the docks, which were too wide for the canals of central England, transferred their loads onto narrowboats. Even into the early 20th century, 20,000 narrowboats loaded up here each year. Suddenly, the canal–river is green with healthy brambles and unrestrained vegetation, until it becomes a stretch bordered by office blocks, from which office-workers spill at sunny lunchtimes to eat their sandwiches on the grassy canal banks.

At the next lock, Clitheroe's (named after a former Sheriff of Middlesex and owner of nearby Boston Manor Park), look to the far side of the canal–river, where there's a glimpse of the old river in its near-natural state bypassing the canal. This usefully channels overflow water from above the upper lock gate. For a time, the canal is hemmed in by railway tracks, the A4 road and the M4 motorway.

Cross the river at the iron Gallows Bridge, which may have been built by Thomas Telford (1757–1834), another of those great 19th-century engineers. The bridge, which bears the Grand Union Canal Company insignia, has a rough surface to enable canal horses to grip it and takes its name from a nearby gallows where highwaymen were hanged. Willow trees and meadow flowers soothe the eye, but the roar of the motorway is never far away and the din of an overhead train may intrude as you pass under a mainline railway bridge. Once you've finally passed beneath the motorway, which has been your companion for too long, peace falls and

Opposite: Purple loosestrife provides a vibrant splash of colour to the muddy backwater of the River Thames behind Brentford Ait, just upstream of Kew Bridge and along the path called The Hollows.

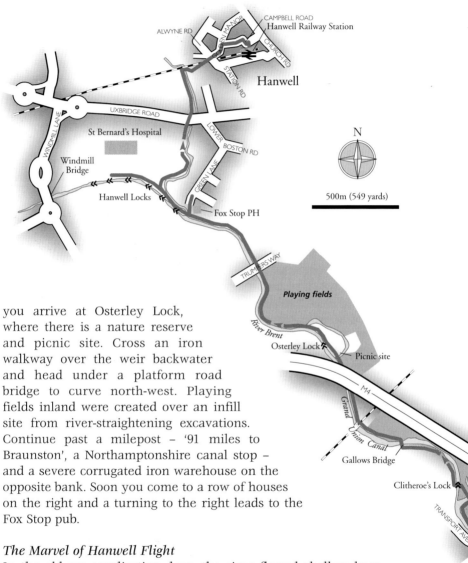

you arrive at Osterley Lock, where there is a nature reserve and picnic site. Cross an iron walkway over the weir backwater and head under a platform road bridge to curve north-west. Playing fields inland were created over an infill site from river-straightening excavations. Continue past a milepost – '91 miles to Braunston', a Northamptonshire canal stop – and a severe corrugated iron warehouse on the opposite bank. Soon you come to a row of houses on the right and a turning to the right leads to the Fox Stop pub.

The Marvel of Hanwell Flight

In the old pre-canalization days, the river flowed shallow here, and cattle crossed over to Green Lane towards Hanwell village. Soon the unnavigable river joins the canal, and you reach the pièce de résistance of the walk: the Hanwell Locks – a 'flight' of locks, which was completed in 1796 and is now a designated ancient monument. A flight is the collective term for a number of locks that take a canal over a steep gradient. A set of locks even steeper than the 53 feet (16m) over ⅓ mile (0.5km) flight at Hanwell is known as a staircase. The locks are indeed like a series of stepped chambers, filled or emptied in succession to raise or lower the boats to the next level. It's easy on foot, but can take a canal boat over 1½ hours to negotiate the full flight of six locks. Each lock chamber has gates at either end; the water level in the chambers is adjusted by opening and shutting paddles over the holes in the gate and in the ground paddle, which spans the width of the lock at the bottom. When a chamber is empty, you can see the culverts through which water from the upper level will gush to fill the next level down.

Keep an eye open for the numbers of the locks, and cross over Lock 97 to the restored side pond. Side ponds are cisterns that store water for topping up the locks – for a single chamber might consume 50,000 gallons (227,000 litres) of water as it fills. Some of the side ponds are covered with a billiard-table film of weed in summer, which has the effect of deoxygenating the water, and there are health-hazard signs to dissuade you from taking a dip. Nevertheless, it is hard to imagine now, but at the end of the 19th century, pollution was so bad along this stretch of the canal that barges were ploughing through lumps of raw, black, gaseous sewage and stirring up foul-smelling silt from the canal bed. Barge men complained that they could not bear to eat on board when cruising through the Hanwell area.

The high wall bordering the right of the towpath after Lock 94 enclosed the former County Lunatic Asylum, which opened in the 1830s. In its day the asylum was innovative in its treatment of psychiatric patients: nursing staff were appropriately trained and paid, and patients were treated with affectionate care and attention. In the hospital's 44 acres

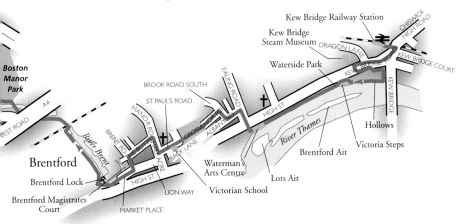

(18 hectares) of land there was a brewery, a bakery and a farm where patients cultivated the land, making the hospital self-sufficient in fruit, vegetables and meat. The hospital also had its own canal-side dock, where surplus produce was shipped to London markets and coal was unloaded for the hospital boilers. The ghost of the former dock entrance can be seen in the form of a low-level concrete-covered arch in the brick wall; the rectangular holes just before it were for fire hoses. On the opposite bank, at Lock 93, is a canal pound and at Lock 96 there is an early 19th-century lock cottage, from which the keeper checked that the locks and traffic were operating smoothly.

On from the Flight

After the sixth lock, the canal narrows to pass under Windmill Lane. This is the site of the last major project undertaken by the Victorian engineer Isambard Kingdom Brunel (1806–59), and is a combination of road, canal and rail routes. Each of the three routes enters the intersection point at a different angle and at a different level: Brunel's metal-beamed trough, which you can see above the towpath, carries the road, while he designed huge brick arches to support the Great Western Railway through a cutting underneath both road and canal.

Retrace your steps back down the flight of locks and take the path left at Lock 96, where canal and original river separate. Your walk continues along a leafy stretch of the real River Brent. Pass under the bridge or cross the Uxbridge Road. Opposite are allotments; in the past the meadows were common land with thriving watercress cultivation. Continue along the west bank of the river towards Brunel's magnificent Wharncliffe Viaduct (see pages 125–29, *Ribbon of Green* walk). Cross the footbridge just before the viaduct and turn right. Turn right again and left into a little park. Turn left under the viaduct arch, right along Golden Manor, right again and follow Campbell Road right to Hanwell Railway Station.

Weeping willow

SHORT CUTS TO LIMEHOUSE: LIMEHOUSE CUT AND HERTFORD UNION CANAL

Summary: Limehouse Basin is where the inland canals meet the River Thames and the world beyond. We take a circular route from the basin to follow a couple of former short cuts for trade and cargo: the Limehouse Cut, between the River Lea and the Thames, which bypasses the loop round the Isle of Dogs, and the Hertford Union Canal. The area has seen better – and worse – times, but it is steeped in industrial history. Much of the path is gravel and/or concrete and, although the route might be a bit grim on a grey day, this is an all-weather walk.

Start and Finish:	Limehouse DLR Station
Distance:	6 miles (10km)
Refreshments:	Narrow Street pub, Limehouse; Palm Tree pub, Mile End

From Limehouse DLR Station, go down the steps above a garden centre and cross into Bekesbourne Street opposite, passing terraced houses on the right. Cross over a footbridge to the pink and cream brick building with red paintwork. This is the approach to the four-lane Limehouse Tunnel, which runs under the Limehouse Basin and was completed in 1994. Follow Horseferry Road round to the right and turn left along Narrow Street. At the end of Sun Wharf warehouses on the right, turn right down an alley to a broad sweep of the Thames. Turn left and follow the Thames Path to the Narrow Street pub and dining-room overlooking the entrance of Limehouse Basin. This Georgian-style building is in fact Edwardian (*c.* 1905–10), and was once the dock's Custom House.

The riverfront here was already bustling by Tudor times. It was the age of exploration, and Sir Walter Raleigh (1552–1618) sailed from Limehouse

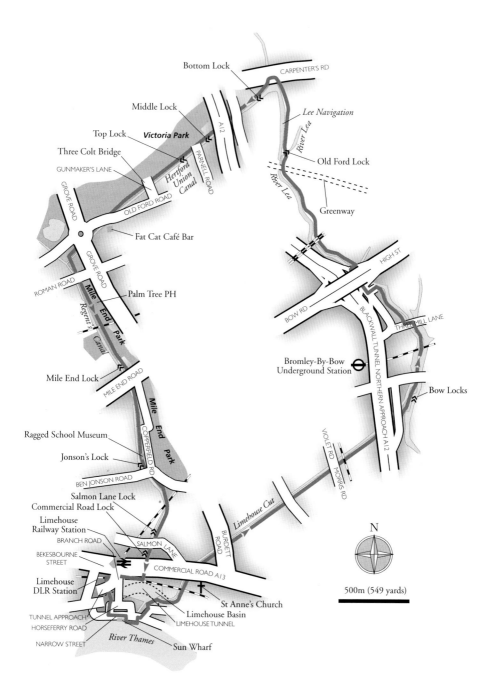

Bottom Lock

CARPENTER'S RD

Middle Lock

Lee Navigation

River Lea

Top Lock

Victoria Park

Three Colt Bridge

Old Ford Lock

GUNMAKER'S LANE

A12

PARNELL ROAD

River Lea

Hertford Union Canal

OLD FORD ROAD

Greenway

GROVE ROAD

Fat Cat Café Bar

GROVE ROAD

HIGH ST

ROMAN ROAD

Palm Tree PH

BOW RD

BLACKWALL TUNNEL NORTHERN APPROACH A12

THREE MILL LANE

Mile End Park

Regent's Canal

Bromley-By-Bow
Underground Station

Mile End Lock

MILE END ROAD

Bow Locks

Mile End Park

VIOLET RD

MORRIS RD

Ragged School Museum

COPPERFIELD RD

Jonson's Lock

BEN JONSON ROAD

Salmon Lane Lock

Limehouse Cut

Commercial Road Lock

Limehouse
Railway Station

BURDETT ROAD

BRANCH ROAD

SALMON LANE

N

BEKESBOURNE
STREET

COMMERCIAL ROAD A13

Limehouse
DLR Station

500m (549 yards)

TUNNEL APPROACH

St Anne's Church

HORSEFERRY ROAD

Limehouse
Basin

Limehouse
Basin

LIMEHOUSE TUNNEL

NARROW STREET

River Thames

Sun Wharf

in 1595 on a quest to the New World and the gold it was rumoured to harbour.

The name Limehouse hails from the 14th century, when lime kilns were worked nearby. Stone was burned and reduced to quicklime powder, which was used in building mortar and, later, for making pottery and as a disinfectant. The constant traffic of sailors from around the world created a cosmopolitan community, including London's first Chinatown, which grew up nearby in the mid-19th century and became notorious for its opium dens. In Victorian times the area was overcrowded, insanitary and dangerous.

Regent's Canal Dock

Go round the Narrow Street pub and up some steps to the road; turn right to cross the entrance to Limehouse Basin and turn immediately left, signposted Limehouse Cut, Lea Valley Walk and Three Mills.

Regent's Canal Dock – as Limehouse Basin was known before 1969 – was excavated from marshy, low-lying land in the 1820s. Instead of today's prospect of desirable waterside residences, the dock was crammed with coasters, short-haul sea-trading ships and lighters that had 'lightened' the loads of ocean-going vessels moored downriver; quays were lined with wharves and warehouses and peopled with gangs of coal-whippers, porters, stevedores and bargees. You could walk directly across the dock using the barges, so tightly were they packed. Coal, iron, grain and timber were among the raw materials and supplies that came via the Thames and London's bigger docks to be transferred to canal barges and narrowboats at Limehouse. The canal boats left the dock in the north-east corner to join the Regent's Canal and on to deliver their goods to north and west London and the Midlands.

From the late 18th century, and before railways took over in the second half of the 19th century, canals provided the cheapest, most efficient method of transporting bulky goods. At their peak in the late 18th century, there was a 4,250-mile (6,840-km) network of navigable rivers and canals, linking centres of production and industry throughout Britain. Despite competing road and rail transport, the Regent's Canal and the dock were still in use in the 20th century, but the dock's commercial life had fizzled out more or less completely by 1969 and its name changed to Limehouse Basin. The area was neglected and rundown until the early 1980s, when the British Waterways joined forces with London Docklands Development Corporation in a regeneration programme.

As you round the first corner of the basin, look straight ahead across the water. In the gaps between the tall block of flats to the right is the tower of a Catholic church, which is topped by a statue of Jesus instead of the usual cross. To the left, a brick accumulator tower marks the coming of hydraulic power, developed by William Armstrong (1810–1900) in 1846. Heavy steam-powered iron cylinders inside the tower maintained the water pressure that provided power to operate the dock's lock gates, a swing bridge and cranes. Locks maintained a constant water level in the dock, as the level of the Thames fluctuated with the tides.

Continue along the brick path round the basin, keeping to the lower path and passing under the iron bridge. At the junction turn left under another footbridge, following signs for Limehouse Cut and River Lea Valley. Ahead is St Anne's Church, completed in 1724 to a design by Nicholas Hawksmoor (1661–1736), one-time clerk to Sir Christopher Wren (1591–1650) and later architect of many distinctive City churches. The church's size and striking tower not only reflected Limehouse's wealth and status at the time, but also served as a landmark for mariners en route to the Pool of London.

Along the Cut

Walk along Limehouse Cut for a rather featureless and relentlessly straight 1½ miles (2.5km), unrelieved by passing traffic which might have added interest in its heyday – but at least the foul-smelling effluents are no longer present. Overcrowding in the city centre and mid-19th-century pollution laws forced factories to relocate, and this is one of the places they came to, making good use of the canal to transport their goods, bring in coal supplies and dump their waste. Limehouse Cut fared worse than other areas, with gas works and chemical-processing factories, lime works and pet-food manufacturers. The bridge beneath the chemical works was known as Stinkinghouse, a description that could probably have applied to the whole stretch. A local recalls his great uncle loading his barge with fish guts discarded from Billingsgate Fish Market and rowing along the Cut to deliver his strong-smelling cargo to the pet-food factory. Anyone who fell in the cut was likely to contract a nasty, if not fatal, water-borne disease.

The original purpose of the canal was to provide a short cut between the River Lea to the east and the Thames at Limehouse. This convenient route, which bypasses the Isle of Dogs' meander in the Thames, was actually planned in the late 16th century during Elizabeth I's reign, though the cut was finally dug only in 1776. Even then it was still something of a

Opposite: Before a backdrop of Canary Wharf's skyscrapers, a red-brick ven-tilation shaft of a Victorian sewage system proudly represents the industrial past of the Regent's Canal, not far from the canal's outlet at Limehouse Basin.

novelty: the pioneering Bridgwater Canal from Wigan to Manchester had been completed just a few years before. Originally, the cut led straight to the Thames at Limehouse, but in 1968 it was diverted to Limehouse Basin. Today, the Victorian factories have gone, and what we now see is the odd surviving, grubby warehouse, office buildings, housing and the occasional decorative steel pier built in the form of a ship's bows – certainly some improvement on the cut's noxious past. Look out for rafts of aquatic plants and an interesting variety of floating nesting boxes to attract waterfowl; some boxes have ramps or slides, others have gabled roofs. You will certainly see moorhens, and you may spot a cormorant.

The Lea Meets the Lee

After about 20 minutes of walking along Limehouse Cut, under the A12 you reach a boardwalk path which leads to the meeting with the Lee Navigation. Cross a stepped bridge over Bow Locks and walk through a welcome green ribbon of an island between the Lee Navigation and Bow Creek. Go left under the railway bridge, beneath Three Mill Lane. On your right is the Three Mills complex (see pages 130–136, *Harnessing the Tide* walk), which used the pull of the tide to power a flour mill and distillery. Continue along the west bank of the Lee Navigation.

The River Lea, in its natural state, wound a leisurely 70-mile (117-km) path from its source near Luton to the River Thames at Bow Creek, downriver of the Isle of Dogs. The waterway was deep enough for Danish invaders to sail up as far north as Hertford in AD 896, but there they became stuck, for King Alfred the Great had split the main stream of the Lea into three channels, which were too shallow for navigation. There is a long history of waterborne trade on the river, too: malt and corn were transported from Hertford in flat-bottomed barges, which had to negotiate the river's uneven, long-winded and inefficient course. In the 16th century, the first section of the Lee Navigation was cut, and locks were built resulting in a direct, reliable and navigable waterway.

Many local farmers and carriers who carted their goods by road felt so threatened by the cheaper water transport provided by the Lee Navigation that they sabotaged river banks, locks and towpath bridges. But the die was cast, and the system of straight channels and locks was extended to include Limehouse Cut in the 18th century. A rash of factories set up along the new waterways, which could now receive raw materials from London and dispatch their finished goods with ease. By the 20th century, barges were taking coal to Hackney Power Station, timber to furniture factories beyond Tottenham, copper to small-arms factories upriver at Enfield (home of the Lee Enfield rifle) and oranges to marmalade factories at Ware. It wasn't until the 1950s that such traffic ceased.

Cormorant

Bazalgette and Duckett

Now the Lee Navigation towpath is bordered with buddleia and dog rose, but the route leaves the towpath just before the next major road (the A11). Turn left, through what appear to be private factory premises but aren't, then turn right to cross two lanes of the A11/Bow Flyover. Look out for the narrow but waymarked return to the towpath. As it passes beneath the A11, the path crosses to follow the navigation's east bank, a leafy stretch with creamy eglantine accompanied by an unwelcome invader, Japanese knotweed.

Just past the sign for the Greenway, you pass under a bridge of metal girders carrying a giant pipe, which is a sewer of 1860s vintage. Greenway is the genteel modern name for the path that follows the route of the Northern Outfall Sewer. This sewer intercepted raw waste from a million households and industries which had once gone straight into the Thames, often bubbling up through the floorboards of poorer homes en route. Salmon and swans disappeared from the Thames, and bodies salvaged from the wrecked *Princess Alice* (see page 76) were covered in vile slime. Outbreaks of cholera were common. In 1858, the year of 'The Great Stink', curtains in the Houses of Parliament were soaked in disinfectant every day to combat the stench rising from the river. It was a man born in Enfield, in the Lea Valley, who solved the problem. Joseph Bazalgette (1819–91) Chief Engineer to London's Metropolitan Board of Works and the brains behind the Victoria and Albert Embankments (see pages 149–158, *Bridging the Thames* walk), oversaw the construction of 1,300 miles (2,170km) of sewer pipe with back-up settling tanks and pumping stations.

Pass the old warehouses on the left bank and turn left over a footbridge across the Old River Lea, signed Old Ford Lock. As the name suggests, this is the site of a river crossing dating from Roman times, on the route between London and Essex. Turn right from the footbridge to continue along the Lee Navigation until the next footbridge, which you cross. Turn left to go back on yourself along the opposite bank for a short distance. Then turn right along the Hertford Union Canal, which is as straight as a die and 1¼ miles (2.1km) long. The canal is also known as Duckett's Cut, after the man who funded it, Sir George Duckett. It was opened in 1830, enabling the tidal River Lea to be bypassed altogether and creating a direct link between the Regent's and Grand Union canals and the Lee Navigation. However, the canal diverted precious water from the Regent's Canal and was closed during the 1850s, although it was later added to the Regent's Canal network.

London's First Park

Because of the low level of traffic on the Hertford Union (see pages 36–41, *Barges Go West* walk), its locks are single: only one boat could go through at a time, unlike the two-way system of twin locks that was a feature of the Regent's Canal, which you will soon meet. You pass Bottom and Middle locks, and then, just before the Parnell Road Bridge (also known as Homerton Footpath Bridge), is the attractive – and rare – Top, or Upper, Lock. It has two sets of double wooden gates, the lower of which has unusual and quite fragile cast-iron balance beams; the beams are infilled with concrete and have reinforcing iron bands. The lock cottages were built at the same time as the canal.

Beyond the Parnell Road Bridge, the houses on the far bank may not be particularly special to look at, but they enjoy a prospect of both the canal and of London's oldest public park. Victoria Park was laid out in 1840, at the beginning of the eponymous queen's reign. Look down to the water for relief from more residential development to nesting rafts for moorhens and ducks, then pass by older properties with canal-side gardens and a Victorian school with an ornate weathervane. The next bridge you pass under is Three Colt Bridge, also known as Gunmaker's Lane Bridge. As with Parnell Bridge, it owes the extra effort taken over its design to being part of the Victoria Park development and is listed for conservation.

Continue beneath Old Ford Road and Grove Road; opposite are 19th-century warehouses converted into the Fat Cat Café Bar. At the junction with the Regent's Canal, turn left. The cobbled track over the bridge gave barge horses a grip on the slopes – maybe sparks flew from a combination of effort and iron shoe, for the cobbles were known as 'scorchers'. As you walk along this part of the Regent's Canal, look for the occasional cutaway canal edge, where there are cobbled ramps beneath the water which a horse could scramble up if it fell in. Perhaps to limit the possibility of such an accident happening and to avoid traffic jams, it was illegal to let horses drink from the canals; instead, water troughs were provided at points away from the towpath.

Changing Landscapes

Now, as you pass through Mile End, you will see canal-side landscapes of varying success, from urban parks with overcrowded flowerbeds to wilder nature reserves complete with ponds, and a possible pub stop at the Palm Tree pub. Once there were factories here producing chocolates, shirts, chemicals and lime juice, but now there are only vast, deserted, green corrugated-iron warehouses overhanging the canal for loading ships under shelter.

At Mile End Lock, neglected cottages are boarded up on the opposite bank, just before Mile End Road crosses the canal. You can take a parallel route through the bordering Mile End Park, for on the opposite bank there is little to see for a time but old warehouses and offices. Soon, you will see the landmark of Canary Wharf Tower in the distance, a vibrant contrast to the abandoned air of much of this stretch.

Just off to the left, in Copperfield Road, is the Ragged School Museum. In 1895, this building was the largest of Dr Barnardo's 148 Ragged Schools in London and gave free lessons to poor children and free meals in winter. The red-brick chimney on your left soon after this point was built in 1906 as a ventilation shaft to air the low-level sewer which extended from the western suburb of Hammersmith and linked up with Joseph Bazalgette's great Northern Outfall Sewer.

A run of locks starts with Jonson's Lock just before Ben Jonson Road, then Salmon Lane Lock, with its lock cottages and tubular footbridge – giant pipes running beneath Commercial Road Bridge – and the Commercial Road Lock. You will see a viaduct, which was designed by George Stephenson (1781–1848), the man who introduced the public to steam trains with the *Rocket* in 1829. The viaduct opened in 1840 and was one of the first railways to connect to the London docks; it now carries part of the Docklands Light Railway system. The section over the canal was roofed to eliminate the possibility of the steam trains passing overhead showering sparks onto barges and setting fire to their cargo.

The canal reaches its destination in Limehouse Basin. Turn right and follow the basin's north side. Look to your left to see the moored narrowboats, which are colourful, clean and for leisure use only. Cross Branch Road and return to Limehouse DLR Station.

BARGES GO WEST: REGENT'S CANAL, MILE END– CALEDONIAN ROAD

Summary: We follow an imaginary coal barge on the first leg of its journey along the Regent's Canal to Paddington Basin, where its load will be transferred to a narrowboat and taken on to Birmingham. The canal created a vital link between the River Thames and London's docklands at Limehouse Basin and the canal network of central England. Our destination is the Canal Museum, where you can see model boats, archive films about working life on the waterways and many artefacts.

Start:	Mile End Underground Station
Finish:	King's Cross Underground and Railway Station
Distance:	4$\frac{1}{3}$ miles (7.2km)
Refreshments:	Mile End, pubs at road level above canal; small café at the Canal Museum

The Regent's Canal was constructed between 1812 and 1820 to connect the Thames at Limehouse to Paddington Basin, the terminus of the Grand Union Canal (see pages 14–19, *Hay and Bricks* walk). Our imaginary coal barge has loaded up at Limehouse Basin, and is on its way along the 8$\frac{1}{2}$-mile (14.2-km) Regent's Canal to join the Grand Union Canal at Paddington Basin. Broad, flat, unadorned and begrimed with coal dust, the barge has an oblong hold for most of its length, filled end-to-end with conical piles of coal. We join its journey at Mile End Lock.

A Barge Reverie
From Mile End Station, turn left and join the canal at the access point on the north side of Mile End Road. Turn right along the towpath to Mile End

Opposite: *Many warehouses along the Regent's Canal beyond Mile End have been converted into desirable waterside residences and offices, but in the canal's heyday horses would have trudged the towpath hauling barges laden with coal.*

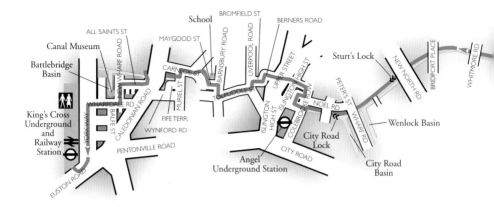

Lock and go under a railway bridge; there are old warehouses jutting over the canal's left bank and shortly afterwards, on the right, is the Palm Tree pub.

In the canals of central England, 7-foot-wide (2-m) narrowboats dominated the older, narrower canals, but here, on the Regent's Canal, barges were more common. They were short-haul carriers and no valuable cargo space was taken up with living cabins or engines; as the barges were also double the width of narrowboats, they had four times the weight capacity – up to 100 tons. One bargeman steered, while a second looked after a horse, which hauled a barge along the straight, smooth waters of a canal and could move around 50 times the weight of a horse-drawn wagon on an unmetalled road. Canal horses needed around 8lbs (3.5kg) of oats a day to maintain energy levels, so a nosebag or bowl was slung around the animal's neck so that it could feed while plodding along. Canal horses also had to be shod every two weeks – twice as often as other working horses. Medium-sized cobs were the usual choice of animal, as they were densely built and strong but small enough to go under the canal bridges.

Some barges towed 'butties' to double their cargo space, although from the mid-19th century these were sometimes hauled along in a long train by a steam tug and from the 1950s by a small tractor on the towpath. Nevertheless, horses were still seen working on the Regent's Canal as late as the 1950s.

Continue heading north along the towpath, with Mile End Park to your right, go under a wide road bridge, keeping straight ahead at the junction with the Hertford Union Canal (see pages 27–35, *Short Cuts to Limehouse* walk), which comes in from the right. Immediately after the bridge is Old Ford Lock (not to be confused with Old Ford Lock on the Lee Navigation). If our coal barge encountered another boat coming in the opposite

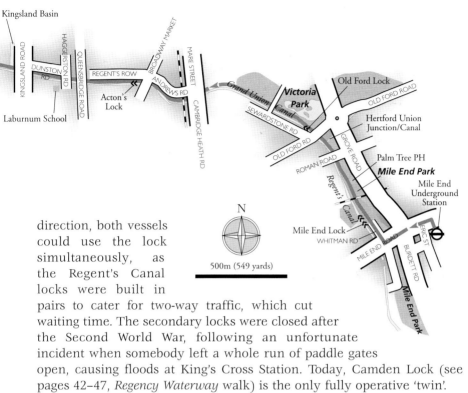

Kingsland Basin

HAGGERSTON ROAD

KINGSLAND ROAD

DUNSTON RD

QUEENSBRIDGE ROAD

REGENT'S ROW

BROADWAY MARKET

ANDREW'S RD

MARE STREET

Acton's Lock

Laburnum School

CAMBRIDGE HEATH RD

Grand Union Canal

SEWARDSTONE RD

OLD FORD RD

ROMAN ROAD

Victoria Park

Old Ford Lock

OLD FORD ROAD

GROVE ROAD

Hertford Union Junction/Canal

Palm Tree PH

Mile End Park

Mile End Underground Station

Regent's Canal

Mile End Lock

WHITMAN RD

HENRIC ST

MILE END ROAD

BURDETT RD

Mile End Park

N

500m (549 yards)

direction, both vessels could use the lock simultaneously, as the Regent's Canal locks were built in pairs to cater for two-way traffic, which cut waiting time. The secondary locks were closed after the Second World War, following an unfortunate incident when somebody left a whole run of paddle gates open, causing floods at King's Cross Station. Today, Camden Lock (see pages 42–47, *Regency Waterway* walk) is the only fully operative 'twin'.

From Old Ford Lock is a lovely stretch of the walk, which is bordered by Victoria Park on the right and warehouses – one of which has its 'legs' in the water – on the left. As you pass under the bridges en route, look out for the metal reinforcements on the corners – these protected the brickwork from being worn by tow ropes. Look down into the water, too, for there are many submarine ramps in cutaway sections of the canal bank, designed for horses to climb up should they fall in. At Mare Street, where brick arches conceal heavy metal girders, there is an iron ring that once supported a rubbing pole for the towing ropes to turn round.

Freshly painted gasometers rise ahead. Gasworks and canals went together, because of the ready supply of prodigious quantities of coal needed to produce the gas. You begin to get an idea of how and why 19th-century London had blackened buildings and a serious pollution problem.

Soon, after a green-painted bridge, you reach Acton's Lock, with its lock-keeper's cottage. On the wall on the right, sadly defaced and damaged mosaics herald our approach to Laburnum School – the tall Victorian building on the left. Under the Haggerston Road bridge, look back to see a mosaic of a laburnum tree, which was made by former pupils. Next comes Kingsland Road, where there's a white rubbing post and where tropical grasses have been found growing: exotic plants are quite often found beside canals, self-grown from seeds attached to passing cargoes from foreign fields. There are factories on the left and you cross a cobbled bridge over the entrance to Kingsland Basin.

More horse ramps appear on the canal bank, and just before the Whitmore Road bridge there is an attractive row of two-storey warehouses. If you look up just after passing the former Rosemary Works, which produced stationery, and a girdered railway bridge, there's a large pipe on which the faded traces of rainbow colours can be seen, even though it's a sewer pipe. Carry on, past Sturt's Lock and a classic Victorian factory chimney on the left, which contrasts with a gleaming white factory building. Carry on past the canal-like cut of Wenlock Basin. Wenlock Basin heralds the approach of the main concentration of warehouses on the Regent Canal.

Just after Wharf Road, City Road Basin opens out on the left. This basin was the canal's main centre for the transferral of goods, such as timber, paper, flour, marble and rubber to the specialist warehouses and factories that lined the quays. Our imaginary barge might have stopped here overnight, as there were stables for the horses. The base of a modern office block curves right down into the water, blocking part of the paired lock.

A Spot of Legging

The towpath comes to an end just before the Islington Tunnel. We, like the canal horse, must go overland, while barges were 'legged' through the tunnel. It was handy if there was someone who could lead the horse, for two men were needed to push their legs against the side walls of the tunnel and 'walk' the barge along. They lay, backs down, on boards that were hooked across the sides of the barge. The journey of more than half a mile (835m) took over an hour and, if motorized narrowboats were also using the tunnel, the leggers were in danger of being overcome by fumes. Nevertheless, even when a steam tug was introduced in 1826 to tow the barges through, many still preferred to 'leg' it rather than pay for the tug.

Turn right to go up to Colebrooke Row, with its tall Georgian terraces. Kink right and left, following signposts for Regent's Canal Bypass West, and then turn right again to go behind an antiques mall. Turn left to Islington High Street and then turn right. Cross the high street and turn left at the Business Design Centre into Berners Road. Keep left, heading round the corner, then turn right into Bromfield Street. Turn left, then right to go past a supermarket, then cross Barnsbury Road. Take a right and then a left into Maygood Street. At the end of the street, take the narrow footpath and follow the school playground round to the right. The path emerges by the Duchess of Kent pub; go straight down and turn left into Muriel Street. Look out on the right for the iron gates as these mark the return to the canal towpath.

Continue to the Caledonian Road bridge, go under it and turn right to go up to the road, then right again to cross the canal. Take the first right, then turn left to see the Canal Museum on the right. The museum itself is in a warehouse that used to store ice. In pre-refrigeration days, ice was big business on the Regent's Canal. Large blocks of ice were cut from Norwegian fjords, carried in the holds of sailing ships to the Thames and transferred to barges in the Regent's Canal Dock (Limehouse Basin); from there, the ice was transported to the warehouse in Battlebridge Basin, which the museum overlooks. Here, overseen by former ice-cream maker Carlo Gatti, it was unloaded into deep wells with sandy floors through which the meltwater filtered.

To reach King's Cross Underground and Railway Station, turn right out of the museum, right along Wharfdale Road and left along York Way. The next walk takes you along the next stretch of the Regent's Canal.

REGENCY WATERWAY: REGENT'S CANAL, CALEDONIAN ROAD–LITTLE VENICE

Summary: In this section of the Regent's Canal route, industry was confined to activity on the waterway itself, for its banks are bordered by some of the most elegant Regency houses in London, rather than warehouses and factories. We pass through trendy Camden, skim past London Zoo and Regent's Park and wander through Little Venice, gaining insight into how canals were built and into an ambitious bit of Regency town planning.

Start:	King's Cross Railway and Underground Station
Finish:	Paddington Railway and Underground Station
Distance:	4¼ miles (7.1km)
Refreshments:	Canal Museum café; Camden Lock Market; Paddington Station

From King's Cross Station, turn left into York Way and right into Wharfdale Road. Turn left into New Wharf Road to pass the Canal Museum (see page 41). Turn right, then left across the canal at Caledonian Road. Turn left just after the bridge to join the towpath. You will see immediately Battlebridge Basin, which the Canal Museum overlooks, on the opposite bank. The basin was open for business from 1822, and past industries included beer bottling, a timber yard and warehouses for corn, salt and imported fruit used for making jam and preserves. Its name is a corruption of Broad Ford Bridge, an ancient crossing on the long-lost Fleet River.

Canal and Railway in Tandem
The restored cast-iron Maiden Lane Bridge carries York Way, the busy road that leads north from King's Cross Station. The canal enjoyed a brief renaissance during the Second World War, taking pressure off the overworked railways, and stop gates were installed at this point to prevent water from flooding into the tunnels in the event of the canal being

bombed. The gates would have been lowered to halt the flow of upstream water into the bomb-damaged area, thus reducing the danger of flooding in the two railway tunnels that had been cut far beneath the waterway in 1852 to carry trains to King's Cross. There was a canal extension to the King's Cross goods shed, although it has long been bricked up, and land between the canal and the railway station was once covered in freight yards.

For a time, waterways and railways worked in tandem. Canal extensions were cut to take boats right into the railway depots to deliver building materials for the new warehouses and railway stations, and goods were transferred by crane directly from boat to train. But speedy, cheap rail freight ultimately put an end to the waterways. Only 17 years after the Regent's Canal was completed, the first mainline railway station was opened at Euston, and over the following decades the rail network took over throughout the country, often following the courses of the old canals.

There's now a rather dreary stretch as the canal curves gently round to the right. On the opposite bank, there's relief in the form of Camley Street Natural Park, an example of how a former coal depot and waste dump can be transformed into a delightful nature reserve; access to it, though, is via York Way and Goods Way. St Pancras Lock and Basin follow immediately; the latter, in its industrial past, was a coal wharf and housed overhead tipping chutes from which waste cinders from steam trains were tipped into the barges beneath.

A trio of bridges, steel-clad residences looking like industrial containers and a zig-zag of warehouses provide some interest on the far bank before you reach Hawley Lock, the first of a procession of locks at Camden. Between the double lock of Hampstead Road top lock and Limehouse Basin, a total of 12 locks regulates the water levels over a drop of 86 feet (26m). Pass the middle lock (Hampstead Road) and then walk beneath Camden High Street. Look back at the arch of the bridge where grooves have been worn on the corners by generations of wet, gritty and very abrasive tow ropes. Cast-iron strips were fixed to the vulnerable corners of some bridges, but at Camden a rolling vertical rod was designed to take the weight of rope. It's still there, its damaged surface evidence of occasional problems with the rolling mechanism. Take a break from the canal here to wander around the craft stalls and eateries of Camden Market, the site of a timber wharf until the 1960s. It was a resting spot for the canal horses, too: the former stables have been absorbed into Dingwalls club. There are also information centres for the Regent's Canal and Camden Lock.

From the market, return to the path, which humps over the entrance to a subterranean basin once occupied by a former gin warehouse, and see ahead an odd folly of a building on the opposite bank. This is Pirate Castle, which was built in 1977 to allow local children to make the most of the water. Look down and you will see a horse ramp just beyond the bridge.

The canal flows beneath railway bridges carrying trains to Euston and turns south, with the gardens of fine Victorian houses sloping down to its banks. Then there is what seems to be a junction, but is in fact Cumberland Basin off to the left, which was a servicing point for a nearby hay, meat and vegetable market until the beginning of the 20th century. Turn right beneath the church on the corner, beneath a Victorian bridge with decorative wrought-iron spandrels, and start out on a stretch along the north side of Regent's Park passing some splendid residential architecture.

Nash's Legacy

The need for a canal to bring coal and other essentials into the heart of London and through to the docklands coincided with architect John Nash's (1752–1835) plan for an upmarket garden estate. It was to be constructed on Henry VIII's former royal hunting ground of Marylebone Park. Nash, doyen of stuccoed Neo-classical Regency architecture (including the Mall and Buckingham Palace), also happened to be an investor in the canal. The waterway had to be incorporated into his plans for the Marylebone Estate and so he became its designer, with his assistant, James Morgan, as engineer. Nash originally saw the canal as a water feature cutting through the park, but it was decided that his elegant villas and terraces in their parkland setting and the industrial traffic of the canal were not a desirable mix. This is why the canal sinks between high banks, so that the senses of Regency residents were not offended. It is also why the canal course is rather circuitous. The Prince Regent (later King George IV) gave his name to both the park and the new waterway. The later confusion of names – the stretch you have been walking is also seen as part of the Grand Union Canal – arises from the amalgamation of the Regent's Canal Company with the Grand Junction and Warwick canal companies in 1929 to form the Grand Union Canal.

The sunken course of the canal does not, however, deprive us of glimpses of London Zoo, laid out in 1827 by Decimus Burton (1800–1881). The airy, aluminium-framed aviary, which was designed in 1961 by Anthony Armstrong-Jones (Lord Snowdon), soars above on the right like a network of trapezes and on the opposite bank are pens containing domesticated animals. Midway through the park borders, with cast-iron

Opposite: Since horsedrawn traffic on the Regent's Canal ceased in the 1950s, this stretch of well-maintained, tree-lined towpath between Regent's Park and Little Venice has become popular with walkers.

Doric-style columns, is Macclesfield Bridge, also known as Blow-up Bridge. It is a replica of the original, which was destroyed together with one barge, three men and a horse in 1874 when the barge's volatile cargo of loose sacks of gunpowder and barrels of petroleum exploded.

The next apparent bridge is particularly interesting, for it is in fact an aqueduct channelling the waters of a lost river, the Tyburn, which Nash diverted to fill the ornamental lake in Regent's Park. More houses grace our route, then the towpath passes beneath the railway line that terminates at Marylebone Station. The canal broadens where there was once a wharf from which goods were transferred to the station freight yards.

Camden Market
Regent's Canal
Information Centre

PRINCE ALBERT ROAD

AVENUE RD

London Zoo

Macclesfield Bridge

Regent's Park

WELLINGTON RD

WELLINGTON RD

PARK RD

ST JOHN'S WOOD RD

ABERDEEN PLACE

LISSON GROVE

MAIDA VALE

Maida Hill Tunnel

N

500m (549 yards)

British
Waterways
Office

Little Venice

WARWICK AVENUE

BLOMFIELD ROAD

MAIDA AVENUE

EDGWARE

DELAMERE TERRACE

BLOMFIELD ROAD

Browning's Pool

WESTBOURNE TERRACE
WESTBOURNE RD

WESTWAY A40

Paddington Basin

EASTBOURNE TER

SOUTH WHARF RD

PRAED STREET

Paddington Underground and Railway Station

The Origins of Lord's

Time again now for the bargees to lie on their backs and 'leg' their way through the 272 yards (250m) of Maida Hill Tunnel (see page 40, *Barges Go*

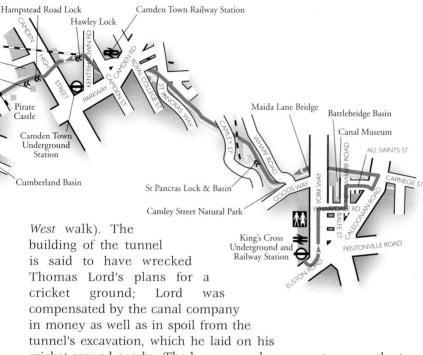

Hampstead Road Lock | Camden Town Railway Station
Hawley Lock
Pirate Castle
Camden Town Underground Station
Cumberland Basin
Maida Lane Bridge | Battlebridge Basin
Canal Museum
ALL SAINTS ST
CARNEGIE ST
St Pancras Lock & Basin
Camley Street Natural Park
WHARFDALE RD
King's Cross Underground and Railway Station
PENTONVILLE ROAD
EUSTON ROAD

West walk). The building of the tunnel is said to have wrecked Thomas Lord's plans for a cricket ground; Lord was compensated by the canal company in money as well as in spoil from the tunnel's excavation, which he laid on his cricket ground nearby. The horses – and we – must go over the top. Go up the steps just before the tunnel and follow a narrow path into Aberdeen Place. Continue to Edgware Road, cross it into tree-lined Blomfield Road and go over Warwick Avenue to pass more admirable Regency houses.

Stop on Warwick Avenue Bridge to look into Browning's Pool, the point at which the old Grand Junction Canal from the Midlands joined up with the new Regent's Canal. The poet Robert Browning (1812–89) lived in nearby Warwick Crescent, hence the basin's name. The cottage just before the bridge on the left was where tolls were levied. If you wish to savour the charm of Little Venice some more, continue over Westbourne Road Bridge, past the British Waterways office, before retracing your steps to Westbourne Road. Cross the road to follow the south side of the basin to the back of Paddington Station, which is clearly signposted. Long before the railway station was built (under the direction of Isambard Kingdom Brunel), Paddington Basin was a thriving inland port and was the terminus of the Grand Junction Canal before the Regent's Canal extension to the London docklands was cut. The Grand Junction had made that first vital connection between the industrial areas of central England and the Thames upstream at Brentford (see pages 14–19, *Hay and Bricks* walk), and the Paddington Basin brought it closer to the heart of London.

GEORGIAN DOCK BOOM: WAPPING–WESTFERRY

Summary: This is one of the longer, more intensive walks in this book, and it is absolutely packed with trading and river history, so allow yourself plenty of time. You will encounter Elizabethan explorers, merchant adventurers and the trading giants behind the first massive dock-building programme of the 19th century, and you will skirt the seedy Limehouse of the Victorian era captured so vividly in the works of novelists Charles Dickens (1812–70) and Peter Ackroyd (b. 1949).

Start:	Wapping Underground Station
Finish:	Westferry DLR Station
Distance:	4 miles (6.7km)
Refreshments:	Various pubs en route, Canary Wharf pier; Pepper Street; Harbour Exchange Square; West India Dock

There is a sense of the fluctuating fortunes throughout the history of this area, which you will see as you trace its evolution from salt-marsh to the thriving docks of the Georgian era and the regenerated Docklands of today. The walk enables you to get your bearings among the dazzling high-rises of Docklands, and to visualize the great docks of the Georgian era. For more details on the Wapping and Shadwell stretches of this walk, see pages 58–64, *Georgian Docks Revisited* walk.

Turn right on leaving Wapping station, where Marc Brunel's Thames Tunnel from Rotherhithe terminated on its completion in 1843 (see pages 100–110, *Wharves and Warehouses* walk). Follow the road as it curves left opposite New Crane Place, then right along Wapping Wall, which marks the course of a former defence against flooding from the tidal Thames. Continue past the 16th-century Prospect of Whitby pub to cross the 1930s red iron drawbridge, which once lifted to allow ships to enter Shadwell Basin (an entrance to the early 19th-century London Docks).

Turn right down the narrow path by the tennis courts into the King Edward Memorial Park. Before the park was opened in 1922, this was an

Opposite: *A giant marker buoy guards the inspiring Museum in Docklands, which occupies part of the 19th-century warehouses that line North Quay at West India Dock.*

area of derelict factories and houses known as the 'brick fields'; from the 1880s it was also the home of Shadwell Fish Market, which was intended to take the pressure off Billingsgate but didn't.

Remembering the Great Adventurers

Stop for a while by an attractive circular building whose ornate ironwork and combination of red brick and white stone belie its function as a ventilation shaft for the Rotherhithe Road Tunnel (see pages 84–90, *Surrey Side Up* walk). An inscribed tablet recalls pioneering adventure and England's quest to discover alternative trade routes to the southern seaways, which were dominated by the Spanish and Portuguese.

From the Thames shore before you, sailed Sir Hugh Willoughby, who was 'frozen unto death' while looking for a north-east passage in 1553; Stephen and William Borough, who were thwarted by ice and bad weather off the northernmost coast of Russia in 1556; and Martin Frobisher (1535–94), who made the first bid for the north-west passage 20 years later. Their ships had towering decks fore and aft and sails billowing from three masts, which was just one of many improvements introduced to ships in the 16th century. The extra masts could carry more complex and efficient rigging, hulls were more stable and the new, stern-mounted rudder increased manoeuvrability. The nearby village of Ratcliff became the victualling centre. The voyages of Willoughby *et al* opened up new opportunities, and over the following decades merchant adventurers formed new trade links; fur and wax came from Russia, while tobacco and sugar came from the New World of the Americas.

Continue along the Thames Path, past two multi-tiered stacks of red-brick apartments and the rather more elegant conversion of *c.* 1795–6 warehouses at Free Trade Wharf. The wharf was built by the East India Company to handle its imports of saltpetre, which was used in gunpowder and to preserve meat. Dutch coasters were still calling at the wharf in the 1970s. The East India Company was founded in 1600 by London merchants who wanted to protect their trading interests in India and the Spice Islands of Indonesia. Over the two centuries that followed, the company became enormously influential in trade and industry, and thus

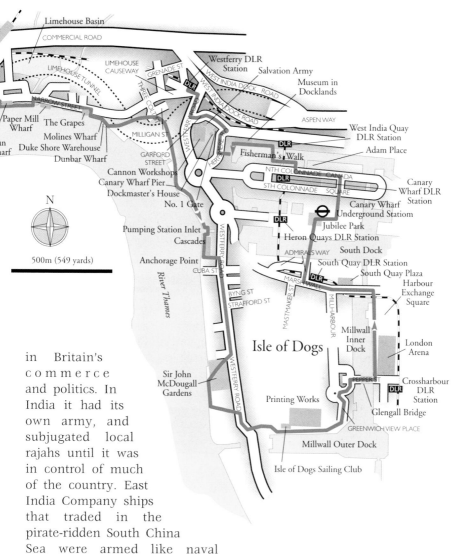

in Britain's commerce and politics. In India it had its own army, and subjugated local rajahs until it was in control of much of the country. East India Company ships that traded in the pirate-ridden South China Sea were armed like naval vessels. For 200 years, the company had a monopoly on valuable goods from the Far East, such as silk, muslin, tea, spices and china. Back in London, the company's influence was evident on both sides of the Thames, where the company built wharves, warehouses, housing for its employees and shipbuilding and repair yards which turned out vessels at the cutting edge of marine technology.

Dickens's Territory

The path heads inland for a stretch to follow Narrow Street, which is lined with warehouses. Turn right down the path at the end of Sun Wharf and then go left to the Narrow Street pub. It is only a brief stretch of riverside path, but the views over the sweep of water round the 'nose' of the Isle of Dogs and the high-rises of Docklands are impressive. You get an idea of how much the peninsula added to a journey's length.

From the pub – a converted dockmaster's house (see pages 27–35, *Short Cuts to Limehouse* walk) – go up some steps and turn right across the entrance to Limehouse Basin. Continue past Paper Mill Wharf and another rash of converted warehouses, which bear no sign of supporting community life. Suddenly, you find yourself in a riverside development of an earlier time, with an early Georgian terrace, which can be distinguished by its shallow-set windows. The artist J.M.W. Turner (1775–1851) is among those who were inspired by this architectural enclave. It was certainly a haunt of the Victorian writer Charles Dickens, who in *Our Mutual Friend* (1866), describes the 16th-century Grapes pub (the 'Six Jolly Fellowship Porters' of the book) as 'a red-curtained tavern that stood dropsically bulging over the causeway'. To sit on the pub's narrow riverside balcony at high tide is as good as being afloat. At one time, a ladder led straight from the balcony to thirsty watermen waiting beneath in their wherries and provided discreet access for stolen and smuggled goods. The pub's reputed custom of getting clients drunk then rowing them out into the river, throwing them overboard and recovering the bodies the next day to sell them for anatomy experiments has happily ceased.

On to the Isle of Dogs

Keep to the right of the leafy gravel square, with its dramatic iron sculpture by Jane Ackroyd of a herring gull standing on a coil of rope. Pass Molines Wharf, with its wall-mounted cranes, and Duke Shore warehouse. 'Shore' is a corruption of the word 'sewer'. We know there was a pottery here in 1660, for the diarist Samuel Pepys (1633–1703) records a visit he paid it. Turn right at the beginning of Dunbar Wharf, signed Canary Wharf and Island Gardens, through the modern residential buildings. The curving tubular footbridge ahead takes you across Limekiln Wharf and onto the Isle of Dogs. This bulbous peninsula is formed by an enormous meander in the Thames. It was always isolated due to marshland to the north and the river to the south, but the Isle of Dogs became a true island when the Georgians launched their first major dock-building programme in the early 19th century. It apparently owes its name to the fact that King Henry VIII kept kennels for his hunting dogs there.

Turn left to go along the left-hand side of Limekiln Wharf, and note the tasteful warehouse conversions, which retain some original features. Lime kilns were introduced to this area in the 14th century and provided an essential ingredient for building mortar. The nearby Limehouse Pottery opened in the 1740s and led the field in producing England's first blue-and-white soft-paste porcelain in a bid to emulate the fine porcelain that was being shipped from China by the East India Company.

Turn right at the end of the wharf, past the curves of Limekiln House and 110 Three Colt Street, a Georgian house with a galleoned coat of arms above its pedimented doorway, and cross Milligan Street to rejoin the riverside path. Robert Milligan (1746–1809), after whom the street is named, was a wealthy West India merchant and shipowner, Jamaican sugar-plantation owner and a founder of West India Dock, which we visit at the end of this walk. Once at the river, look back at a skeletal tower extension to a block of flats that evokes container gantries. Ahead is Canary Wharf Pier and riverside, with plenty of bars and restaurants.

Follow the path round beyond Canary Wharf Pier and go over the footbridge across Pumping Station Inlet, where there's a severe warning to 'Keep Out' because of dangerous tides and pumps starting into action. Tides here have always been a problem: in the 15th century, floods broke down the embankment wall at this spot. When they receded, a 5-acre (2-hectare) inland lake was left behind; it became known as the Poplar Gut and was a busy fishing spot; later, the Gut disappeared under the waters of the West India docks. The embankment was rebuilt further inland and the shore became a temporary storage place for stacks of timber. In the 18th and 19th centuries, the scene was dominated by busy shipbuilding yards. On the corner of the inlet, with its Captain Pugwash-style crow's nest balconies, is the Cascades development, whose design provoked adverse criticism.

Sweet chestnut

The Millers' Tale
The next large-scale condominium is Anchorage Point, at the end of which, beside a closed

riverbus pier, turn left; at Westferry Road, turn right. It is possible that the path will continue along the riverside when current buildings are finished. Carry on along the main road, past an incongruous cluster of small houses and shops, until you see the riverside Sir John McDougall Gardens on the right – an island of undulating green with mature chestnut and plane trees and a vista towards Surrey Docks across the river. Now, in this south-west corner of the Isle of Dogs, you are in Millwall, whose name comes from the group of windmills which stood atop the wide tidal embankment that followed the river between Blackwall and Limehouse. The mills powered corn- and oilseed-grinding machinery, but were made redundant by the coming of steam power. The grain business in Millwall continued to flourish, however, and in 1868 Millwall Dock was opened to provide quays for on-the-spot unloading and processing of grain and timber.

Go to the far right corner of the gardens and continue along the riverside path. All too soon you must return to the road and continue along it until you pass Westferry Printing Works; turn left along the brick-walled and paved path immediately after the entrance, signed Crossharbour DLR Station and London Arena, to walk beneath the towering iron gantries that once supported overhead cranes. The far side of the dock is flanked by monotonous yellow-brick residences, but our route is alleviated by the floating home of the Isle of Dogs Sailing Club, young plane trees and a chimney ahead, which is all that remains of a former factory.

Follow the path to the left beneath two more gantries alongside Millwall Inner Dock, where some Thames sailing barges are moored. Millwall Dock was dominated in the 19th century and well into the 20th (when four pneumatic elevators, a 13-storey granary and silos lined the quays) by the mills of the McDougall family, who were pioneers of self-raising flour. The McDougalls had originally been involved in chemical fertilizers, but when Manchester chemist Alexander McDougall introduced a revolutionary new baking powder, his sons decided to focus on flour-milling. McDougall's mill operated here for nearly 100 years and was a major local employer; it closed in 1982 and was demolished soon after.

Glimpses of the Docks

Turn right into Pepper Street over Glengall Bridge and turn left to pass a floating Chinese restaurant and the now closed London Arena. Dazzling glass rises above black rectangles of water in Harbour Exchange Square, where there are shops, sandwich bars and estate agents. At the road, turn left and carry on past South Quay Plaza and past South Quay DLR Station. Turn right into Admirals Way to South Dock where, to the right, is a surprise vista of the Millennium Dome at Greenwich, which really confuses your sense of direction. Turn right over the dramatic suspension footbridge, and at the far end look left, beyond the modern buildings, to catch a glimpse of a 1909 red-brick pumping station which once sat close to the western end of what was the City Canal. The canal, funded by the Corporation of London and built between 1800 and 1805, seemed like a good idea as it cut across the Isle of Dogs, saving the 3-mile (5-km) round trip by river. It was never much used by ordinary shipping, though, and was sold to the West India Company, which, by 1802, had its own access via new docks just to the north. The canal was subsumed into South Dock, which dealt primarily in timber from the Baltic.

From the suspension bridge, go through the building opposite into Jubilee Place. Just before the glass hemisphere of Canary Wharf Station, turn right into Jubilee Park where water cascades down stepped slabs of grey stone. Turn left at the top to go along Upper Bank Street and take the second left into Canada Square, with its gleaming towers and striking blue elliptical sculpture. At the steel columns of North Colonnade turn right – you actually go through the glass doors – into Adam Place. Follow the waterside left along Fisherman's Walk to reach West India Import Dock, the first of the great Georgian docks, which was built in 1802. Look across to where the Thames-built SS *Robin* is moored; this is a rare surviving example of a 'dirty British coaster with a salt-caked smoke stack', as immortalized by the poet John Masefield in *Cargoes* (1903). Cross the footbridge to the North Quay where just two warehouses have survived. Originally there were nine warehouses, which lined the waterside for half a mile (835m), forming the largest brick building in the world at the time.

An Overworked River

In the late 18th century, new trade routes had led to an increase in shipping, and the ships themselves were increasing in size. Vessels from all over the world were jostling for space on the Thames. Customs failed to keep up and ships queued for weeks to have their cargo weighed and taxed at the overcrowded 'Legal Quays'; security and policing were non-existent and pilfering and corruption were rife. A group of merchants importing from the West Indies joined with plantation owners, ship owners, agents, bankers and Members of Parliament to pressurize the Government into taking notice of their interests. One outcome was the building of the West India Docks, which not only provided a constant level of deep water that could be maintained by locks, but also offered fortress-like security.

A Government promise of a 21-year monopoly on handling coffee, sugar, rum, pimento, cotton and mahogany from the West Indies lured investors, and William Jessop (who was also Chief Engineer on the Grand Junction Canal) was hired as the engineer. Thirty acres (12 hectares) of earth were dug out manually to a depth of 23 feet (7m) for the import dock alone. Wide quays meant that cargo could be discharged under the direction of stevedores – or lumpers, as they were known – direct from the ships to the transit sheds and from there to the warehouses behind. One part of the quay became known as Blood Alley because the workers frequently suffered cuts from carrying rough sacks of brutally sharp sugar cane.

For the first time, ships and cargo were secure behind the high walls that surrounded the whole complex, and there was a 6-foot (2-m) ditch along the outer wall and military-style security. Since 1929, water levels in the docks have been maintained by massive pumps in the impounding station at the west end of South Dock. The original machinery is still used each night, drawing 4 million tons of water into the docks each year – enough to fill them three times over.

The Museum in Docklands

Part of the surviving warehouses is given over to the Museum in Docklands. For an evocative and informative insight into the history of the Thames, London's development as a port and life and work in the docklands this museum is an absolute must. There are reconstructions of a Legal Quay and a 'sailor town' of the 19th century, restored river craft and newsreel footage of historic moments, such as the devastating bombing of the area during the Second World War. By targeting the London docklands, which handled a quarter of the country's imports, the Germans aimed to paralyze London and the country as a whole. In September 1940, a sustained attack by Luftwaffe planes destroyed most of the West India warehouses. Fires fuelled by stocks of inflammable sugar and rubber burned for days on end. The toll on human lives in this area was one of the highest in London. Yet the docks continued to operate throughout the war.

From the museum, cross the quay to turn left at the end of the water and walk through the replica Hibbert Gate (named after former dock chairman George Hibbert). Turn right and right again into Hertsmere Road, opposite the Cannon Workshops. This 1824 building housed engineering workshops and stores, and is named after the small cannon that stood at its entrance. The little circular domed building in front, dating from 1803, was used by the dock police and the Government's Military Guard for storing arms. On the opposite side of the road you can see the defensive walls, complete with spikes and barred windows, of the old warehouses. The red-brick building with a colonnaded porch on the left is the former headquarters of the Port of London Authority's West India Docks police division. Gone were the days when lumpers might conceal tobacco, sugar and other booty in their voluminous, broad-hemmed canvas jackets, for at the gates they might be stopped by police from the dock's own company, customs, city or port authority.

The Demise of the Original Docklands

Turn left at the next building on the left, which is Dockmaster's House. This was built as an excise office between 1807 and 1809, but is now a restaurant. In West India Dock's heyday, however, it overlooked the No. 1 Gate, where the Portland stone piers still stand. This is the point where hundreds of hopeful labourers would turn up for the daily 'call on' in the hope of work. The availability of work on the docks fluctuated because trade in such crops as sugar and tobacco was seasonal and ships' schedules were affected by weather conditions, so dock labourers were hired as needed. A massive increase in trade – sevenfold over the 19th century as a whole – led to the frantic building of warehouses and a great influx of workers, but in the 1880s and 1890s business slumped and there was an over-supply of both. Dock and trading companies, desperate to sell warehouse space and in stiff competition, drastically cut costs – and pay. Once, dock labourers might have been sure of a day's work, but now they were being hired by the half-day or even the hour. A strike to improve working conditions called in 1889 by the Dock Labour Union resulted in the hourly rate increasing from 4d to 5d, but the 'call on' system continued until 1960.

In 1975 the docks were running at a loss of £8 million, and they were closed down the following year. By the late 1970s, 10,000 jobs had been lost in Docklands as a whole, 60 per cent of the water and surrounding land lay empty, and 9,000 local residents left the area. Today, 20 years after the London Docklands Development Corporation began its regeneration programme, a very different sort of life has returned to the area, and international trade is now handled at deep-water berths downstream in the Thames Estuary.

Beyond No. 1 Gate and set back behind a high hedge is the 1888 Salvation Army Hostel, formerly a temperance hostel for Scandinavian sailors. When you meet the main road, turn sharp left, almost back on yourself, into what appears to be an unprepossessing terrace of modern houses. Just beyond them, however, is a row of delightful cottages built in 1819 for the West India Dock Company police. Turn right at the end of Garford Street for Westferry DLR Station, which you will see ahead.

GEORGIAN DOCKS REVISITED: ST KATHARINE DOCKS–SHADWELL BASIN

Summary: Discover the lost – and found – remains of the smaller Georgian docks of the early 19th century. Relive the story of Wapping and Shadwell as they evolved from fishing hamlets into overcrowded, seedy and unsafe areas haunted by sailors, boatbuilders and rope- and sack-makers and later into desirable residential districts for the well-heeled. Some stretches of this route are overshadowed by multi-storeyed 19th-century warehouses, but there are also glimpses of a broad reach of the Thames and the basins and canals are like reflective gems among the dense buildings.

Start and Finish:	Tower Hill Underground and DLR Station
Distance:	3½ miles (5.8km)
Refreshments:	Various cafés and the Dickens Inn at St Katharine Docks; plus other memorable pubs en route

From Tower Hill Station head downhill, following signs for the Tower of London via the pedestrian walkway that goes beneath the busy roads overhead. It's worth a brief detour left to see a section of the London Wall: a single, mighty fortification that once encircled the Roman and medieval cities. You can spot the difference between the Roman wall with its sandstone base and courses of red tiles, and the rough masonry of medieval times, when a further 21 feet (6.4m) was added.

The Last Georgian Dock

When you reach a junction of paths around the remains of a medieval sentry gate, turn left to border the Tower's moat gardens, which were once a defence system filled with Thames water. Go up the steps to cross and turn right along Tower Bridge Approach. Just before the bridge, go down the steps and turn left downstream, past a monstrously ugly concrete hotel complex on your left and the Thames on your right. Enjoy the

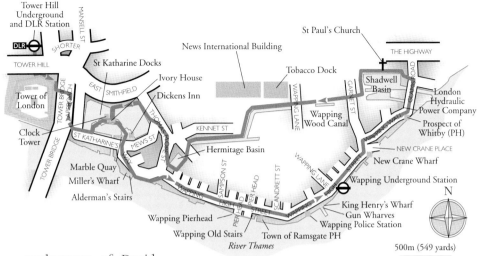

Tower Hill Underground and DLR Station

DLR · TOWER HILL

MANSELL ST
SHORTER
TOWER BRIDGE APPROACH
EAST SMITHFIELD

Tower of London

Clock Tower

TOWER BRIDGE

St Katharine Docks

Ivory House

Dickens Inn

THOMAS MORE ST
ST KATHARINE'S
MEWS ST

KENNET ST

Hermitage Basin

Marble Quay
Miller's Wharf
Alderman's Stairs

News International Building

Tobacco Dock

WAPPING LANE

Wapping Wood Canal

SAMPSON ST

WAPPING HIGH STREET
PIER HEAD
PIER HEAD
SCANDRETT ST

St Paul's Church

THE HIGHWAY

GARNET ST

REARDON
Shadwell Basin

London Hydraulic Power Company

Prospect of Whitby (PH)

WAPPING WALL

NEW CRANE PLACE

New Crane Wharf

WAPPING LANE

Wapping Underground Station

King Henry's Wharf
Gun Wharves
Wapping Police Station

N

Wapping Pierhead
Wapping Old Stairs   Town of Ramsgate PH

River Thames

500m (549 yards)

exuberance of David Wynne's 1973 statue, *Girl with a Dolphin*. Cross the swing bridge across the entrance channel that connects the three basins of St Katharine Docks to the Thames. In the elegant house in front of you lived the Dockmaster; tall windows afforded him an excellent view of boats as they approached along the Thames and entered the docks. The house dates, like the docks themselves, from the early 19th century and is typical of the Georgian Neo-classical style.

Follow the path left, then right at the red drawbridge. St Katharine Docks were designed by the Scottish engineer Thomas Telford, who designed more than a thousand bridges, including the suspension bridge over the Menai Strait. These were the last of the Georgian docks to be built – they opened in 1828 – and they are the closest to the commercial heart of the City. St Katharine Docks were purpose-built to take smaller ships and lighters, which transferred goods from vessels berthed at West India and East India docks further east. In their construction, more than 1,250 houses were cleared and 11,000 people displaced, together with the medieval church of St Katharine, which was founded originally by Queen Matilda in 1147, and for which the dock was named. But the docks' commercial success was short lived, as their capacity and entrance soon proved too small for the new steam and iron ships that were beginning to take over.

Ahead is the Dickens Inn, a former 18th-century brewery warehouse with Elizabethan-style galleries superimposed; but unless you're in need of a pub stop, turn right past Marble Quay – named after the goods it handled – and immediately left along St Katharine's Way. On the left is an early 20th-century red-brick building, which was once a base for the Port of London Authority; on the right, look up at the cranes on the loading doors of Miller's

Wharf warehouses. Pass Alderman's Stairs, the first of many a tempting narrow passage leading to the river – and a dead-end. People gathered on the steps to hail passing clinker-built wherries. Short-haul wherries were manned by a single waterman and those for longer trips by two; cries of 'Eastward ho!' or 'Westward ho!' indicated the wherry's direction.

Historic High Street

Turn right just past the alley for a short stretch of the Thames Path (signed). The riverside then becomes blocked by buildings, so the walk returns inland to follow the part-cobbled Wapping High Street, a route that was created *c*. 1570. Historically, the fishing hamlet of Wapping was isolated, hemmed in by marshy land to the north and the river to the south. According to the 16th-century historian John Stow, Wapping High Street was a 'filthy strait passage, with alleys of small tenements or cottages'. The area became increasingly overcrowded and insanitary as river traffic and its associated trade grew in the 18th and 19th centuries, but today, the mostly 19th-century warehouses have been given a modern makeover and provide smart riverside flats for City workers. Their names, such as Cinnabar, Java and Zanzibar, recall their exotic past.

If you had been walking along Wapping High Street in the 19th century, you would now be passing London Docks on your left. Three times the size of St Katharine Docks, London Docks were excavated between 1801 and 1805 from a mostly urban site that had held glass and rope works and market gardens. The enterprise was rather more successful than St Katharine, partly because of the docks' greater extent, but especially because they enjoyed a 21-year monopoly of trade in any tobacco, rice and wine that came from outside the East and West Indies. However, in 1967, London and St Katharine docks were operating at a loss of £1.25 million. As a result, London Docks closed, and Daniel Asher Alexander's fine 1804–5 multi-storey warehouses, which were known as 'stacks' and lined the North Quay, were demolished.

Part of the site lies beneath the News International buildings, dubbed 'Fortress Wapping' in 1986 when those employees of *The Times, Sunday Times* and *Sun* newspapers who did not support the print unions' call to strike had to be protected as they turned up for work. The small garden at Wapping Pierhead, set between graceful Georgian terraces – the former homes of dock company officials – marks the former entrance to the docks.

Opposite: *On passing the Prospect of Whitby, nip down the passage that runs beside it, as passengers wanting to hail a wherry would have done in the past, and you will find the gallows from which pirates were once hanged.*

Crime and Punishment

Just after the pierhead, it's worth popping into the Town of Ramsgate pub on the right to drink with the ghosts of such luminaries as Captain William Bligh (1754–1817) and Fletcher Christian (*c.* 1764–*c.* 1793) in their companionable days before the mutiny on the *Bounty* in 1787. The Irish adventurer and Civil War Parliamentarian Captain Thomas Blood (*c.* 1618–80) was apprehended here in 1671, clutching the coronation crown of Charles II (flattened with a mallet to make it easier to hide), which he had stolen from the Tower of London.

The adjacent Wapping Old Stairs led to Execution Dock, where crowds gathered in the 17th and 18th centuries to watch the public executions of mutineers and pirates, including, in 1701, naval officer-turned-pirate Captain William Kidd. The hangings took place at low tide and the corpses were then tarred and transferred to a body-shaped cage of banded iron and suspended from a gibbet in the river, to be removed only after three tides had washed over them. The last execution here was in 1830. It was at Wapping Old Stairs, too, that the notorious Judge Jeffreys (1645–89), who condemned more than 300 Royalist rebels to death in his Bloody Assizes of 1685, was captured in his attempt to follow James II into exile via a collier bound for Hamburg.

Later, in the 19th and 20th centuries, oranges and spices were unloaded here. There are still locals here who remember dockers breaking open a crate of oranges each morning and throwing fruit to passing schoolchildren. And the first fuchsia arrived in England via somewhere in Wapping – thanks to a sailor who'd brought a plant back from the West Indies.

After the mellow brick warehouses, the startling white and blue of Wapping Police Station is rather a shock, but shortly after on the right, opposite the park, is the more conservative base of the oldest uniformed police force in the country. Today, the building houses the Marine Support Unit of the Metropolitan Police; the original river police force was set up here in 1798 to deal with the pilfering and corruption that plagued cargo-laden vessels as they queued up at quays to be passed by Customs. Proposed by a magistrate named Patrick Colquhoun, the force was funded by a pressure group of West India merchants (more than half of all losses were sustained by the West India fleet) and the Government. The looting problem was tackled by appointing offical gangs of lumpers (stevedores) to unload the ships and police watermen patrolled the river in wooden rowing boats. Within a year, losses were cut by 80 per cent. Today's unit has a fleet of 15 patrol boats, a command vessel and four rigid inflatables, and is concerned principally with drug importation, terrorism, recovering bodies from the Thames and advising leisure users on safety. Just after the police station are the tall warehouses of King Henry's Wharf and Gun Wharves, which recall the 16th-century site of a foundry that made cannons for Henry VIII's navy.

Shadwell's Place in History

Shortly after Wapping Underground Station, opposite the entrance to New Crane Place – a concentration of storage warehouses at the start of Wapping High Street – curve left, then turn right, into Wapping Wall, so called because it was built over a 1560s sea wall that replaced the medieval flood defences destroyed by heavy tides. Follow the road round to the left, passing the 15th-century Prospect of Whitby, which claims to be London's oldest riverside pub. A board on the front of the building lists the various monarchs whose subjects the pub has served. Notable customers of the past have included diarist Samuel Pepys in the 17th century and the author Charles Dickens in the 19th century. The pub's name actually dates from the late 18th century, when a collier called the *Prospect* from the east-coast port of Whitby was supposedly moored alongside the pub. Nip down the adjacent alley: if the tide's out, you can go down to a stony beach and look back at the balconies and gallows. There's a fine view of Bermondsey and Rotherhithe waterfronts and the warehouses of Butler's Wharf on the opposite, Surrey side of the river, and of Tower Bridge and south-east towards Canary Wharf.

From the pub, follow the road round to the left, just past the 1891 red-brick building, a former London Hydraulic Power Company pumping station. Until 1977, this generated power for the local dock machinery and for commercial buildings in west and central London. Just after the bridge, turn left into Shadwell Basin and walk round its north side past St Paul's Church, known as the Captains' Church because so many sea captains lived or lodged locally in the 18th century. The names of 75 captains and their wives are in the burial register of 1725–95 and the church's founder was connected with the East India Company. The explorer Captain James Cook (1728–79) lived in Shadwell in the 1760s and his eldest son was baptized at St Paul's. The original building fell into disrepair and the church you see today dates from the 1820s.

Now you pass through Shadwell. A beach of gravel among the surrounding mudflats and marshes provided a good landing spot and ensured the village of Shadwell its place in history. A Roman watchtower was built by the shore in the late 3rd century AD as a defence against Saxon pirates, and 'Shade Well' (meaning shallow stream) is mentioned in early medieval records. During Elizabeth I's reign, it was still a fishing hamlet on the lane between the Tower of London and the Manor of Stepney, but with the growth of shipping and trade in the 17th and 18th centuries, the population swelled with sailors and other marine workers. There's another Shadwell in Virginia, USA, which was the home of American president Thomas Jefferson (1743–1826) and named after his mother's birthplace of Shadwell, London.

Smokers' Corner
At the far end of the basin turn left and right to loop round the basin entrance. Take the lower path (signposted St Katharine Docks) along Wapping Wood Canal, whose existence and landscaping saves this strip of upmarket residential development from being completely soulless. After the first short stretch, at the crossing of paths, go more or less straight ahead, past Tobacco Dock. In Victorian times this whole area was taken up by the 35 acres (14 hectares) of London Docks. It was surrounded by courtyards, alleys and the lodging houses of dock labourers, sack-makers and watermen and was overcrowded with poverty-stricken families who scraped their living from the waterside.

Suddenly, and surprisingly amid the relentlessly urban landscape of today, appear two replicas of ships that delivered cargoes to London in the 18th and 19th centuries. This was once the north side of London Docks, and the cast-iron-framed Tobacco Dock warehouse, which was built between 1811 and 1814, still stands, waiting to be reused. You can see the magnificent windows and the 19th-century wood and cast-iron structure of the old tobacco warehouse, once part of a 5-acre (2-hectare) complex. The Docks were also an important wine depot, with 18 acres (7.3 hectares) of vaults beneath the quays, and also stored enormous quantities of wool, spice and ivory.

Shortly after Tobacco Dock, the path turns sharp left; ignore the right turn and keep on until the junction, with some of the original dock wall on the opposite bank. Turn right and continue to steps leading to Hermitage Basin, one of the former dock's entrance basins and now surrounded by yet more desirable residences. Exit by the remains of the old dock gateways and walls and turn right into Thomas More Street and follow it round to the left. Opposite the superstore buildings on the right, take the entrance, left, to St Katharine Docks (signposted), and walk along the right of the dock basin until you reach the main entrance with model elephants on the piers of the gateway. No surprise, then, to see, on your left, Ivory House, once the centre of valuable ivory imports. Turn left just past this to pass beneath the fine clock tower, then right along an arcade of shops to the drawbridge and small round building, which is now a café. Turn right here to walk along the back of the hotel complex, past a historic boat collection that includes Thames barges. Leave the dock and turn right to retrace your steps along St Katharine's Way and the Tower moat path to Tower Hill Station.

BULK CARGO: MUDCHUTE AND ISLE OF DOGS EAST

Summary: A short walk with opportunities for lingering over some classic London riverside views – notably of Greenwich waterfront and of broad reaches of the Thames and its shores beyond Docklands and the City. In the parts where concentrated residential developments get a little tedious, the names of streets and districts evoke a sense of this area's more interesting past.

Start and finish: Island Gardens DLR Station
Distance: 2½ miles (4.2km)
Refreshments: Café at Island Gardens; the Ferry House pub and other pubs and shops in Westferry Road

Scan the river panorama from Island Gardens with a painterly eye, for it is the one on which the 18th-century Venetian artist Canaletto based his 1752 painting *Greenwich Hospital from the North Bank of the Thames*. The reality has not always been as appealing as Canaletto's painting, for this site was nothing more than a waste dump in the 19th century, and unwelcome debris would wash ashore in front of Greenwich Hospital on the opposite bank. It's not surprising, then, that the Admiralty, which took over the hospital for its Naval College, had the area cleared and the park created in 1895 to improve its outlook across the river.

Greenwich River Crossings

From Island Gardens DLR Station, where the Greenwich Foot Tunnel emerges from beneath its glass-domed, red-brick rotunda, turn left into Ferry Street. Cross the street obliquely, keeping Johnson's Drawdock on your left, and continue for a few yards along the street that runs parallel with the Thames. From *c.* 1850, Johnson's Drawdock was one of the few public slipways on the River Thames that could be used by local industries during this period. Small coasters and barges berthed at high tide at drawdocks and unloaded their cargo onto waiting carts at low tide. The site was blocked by a scrapyard for a time until the 1980s, when public access was reinstated as part of the Docklands regeneration and landscaping programme.

Turn left at the sign to the riverside walkway where, directly ahead, across the river, lies the tea clipper *Cutty Sark* in its dry dock at Greenwich. After a few metres along the Thames, return to the road at the early 19th-century Ferry House pub, once the boarding point for the Greenwich Ferry. Customers could watch for its arrival from the pub's tower. There was probably an earlier hostelry on this site, one of a handful of buildings that existed on the southern part of the Isle of Dogs in the 18th century. The opening of Greenwich Foot Tunnel in 1905 – and of the Blackwall Tunnel to the north a few years earlier, in 1897 – served to make the ancient ferry crossings and the Greenwich watermen who operated them redundant. There were ferry services between Greenwich and the Isle of Dogs from at least 1450, initially only for foot passengers; in 1812, when Westferry Road was built, a horse-ferry service was introduced to carry goods, animals and vehicles. Greenwich watermen were appeased by being granted permission to continue carrying foot passengers.

Do not follow the Thames Path signs at this point; instead go left through the iron gates at the side of the Ferry House pub and left to pass in front of the restaurant at the base of a block of flats. If, by any chance, access to this section is barred, go right, left and left again on the road route to get back to the Thames Path.

The Colour Factory

The riverside walk opens to a broad boulevard with rows of plane trees. Just past the trees, look right to the workshops of Burrells Wharf, where, not so long ago, pink-tinted pigeons roosted on the rooftops, their feathers coloured by smoke from The Colour Factory chimneys. The factory manufactured chemical colours until its closure in 1986. The first industries here, in the middle decades of the 19th century, were linked with shipbuilding, but over the following decades these declined. Burrells, who took over the site in 1888, were initially exporters of paints, chemicals, pharmaceutical drugs and oils; they later concentrated on producing paint, dyes and pigments and then, from 1943, focused on chemical colours.

Continue past the workshops until a sunken space filled with great timbers on your right marks the spot where Isambard Kingdom Brunel's

Opposite: The view of the Royal Naval College at Greenwich across the Thames from the Isle of Dogs was one that inspired the Venetian painter Canaletto in the 18th century.

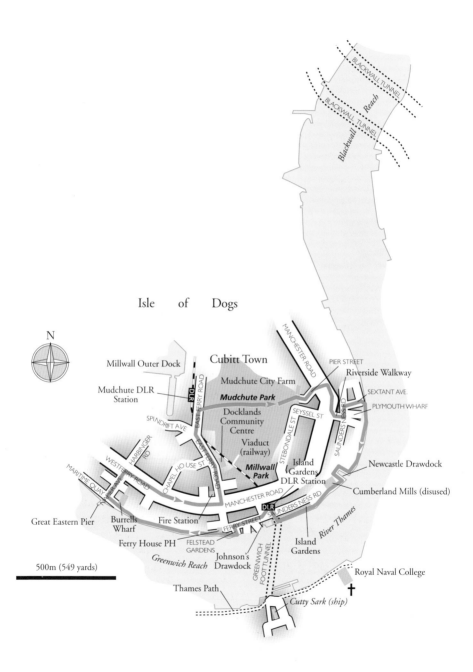

Isle   of   Dogs

Cubitt Town

Millwall Outer Dock

Mudchute DLR
Station

Mudchute City Farm

Mudchute Park

Docklands
Community
Centre

Viaduct
(railway)

*Millwall
Park*

SPINDRIFT AVE.

HARBINGER RD.

WESTFERRY ROAD

MARITIME QUAY

CHAPEL HO USE ST.

EASTFERRY ROAD

FERRY ROAD

MANCHESTER ROAD

SEYSSEL ST.

STEBONDALE ST.

SAUNDERS RD.

PIER STREET

Riverside Walkway

SEXTANT AVE.

PLYMOUTH WHARF

Newcastle Drawdock

Cumberland Mills (disused)

Island
Gardens
DLR Station

Great Eastern Pier

Burrells
Wharf

Fire Station

Ferry House PH

FELSTEAD
GARDENS

Johnson's
Drawdock

Greenwich Reach

FERRY STREET

SAUNDERS NESS RD.

Island
Gardens

River Thames

GREENWICH FOOT TUNNEL

Royal Naval College

Thames Path

Cutty Sark (ship)

N

DLR

DLR

500m (549 yards)

Blackwall Reach

BLACKWALL TUNNEL

BLACKWALL TUNNEL

BLACKWALL TUNNEL

Blackwall

Great Eastern was built; at low tide you can look over the wall to the river shore and see the ridges of the ship's launching ramp. This white elephant of a ship was never commercially viable, but she memorably laid the first transatlantic telegraph cable connecting Britain and America (see pages 91–99, *Millennium Landscape* walk). The wooden piles are thought to mark the 1858 launching site of the ship, which was the largest of its day, unmatched in size and strength for 40 years. The *Great Eastern* was a combination of sailing ship, screw and paddle steamer, able to carry 12,000 tons of coal (enough to reach Australia without refuelling), as well as 800 first-class and 3,000 second-class passengers, or 10,000 troops. She ran at a loss as a transatlantic passenger liner, and had a working life of only 16 years. Two thousand labourers had worked to build her and several were killed in the process; in the course of her construction, both the shipyard and the ship's first owner were bankrupted. At the end of it all, Brunel was a sick man; he died barely a year after the ship's launch and just 10 days after being photographed on its deck.

Cubitt's Mudchute

Turn right just after passing the old shipyard at Great Eastern Pier to walk down Napier Avenue, then turn right again to pass the inland frontage of Burrells Wharf, followed by a rather dull stretch of Westferry Road, the main road that follows the loop of the Isle. Turn left at East Ferry Road, just after Millwall Fire Station, which is Queen Anne in style but actually dates from 1904–1905. A surprise enclave of Victorian houses survives in this area of relentless regeneration and on the right, slicing across Millwall Park, is another relic: the Millwall Viaduct, which was built in 1872 and now carries a Docklands Light Railway line.

Mudchute Park and DLR station are named after the spoil excavated from Millwall Dock in the 1860s, which was carried on chutes to 'settle' in this area. This south-east corner of the Isle of Dogs is known as Cubitt Town, as it was largely developed in the 1850s and 1860s by William Cubitt (1785–1861), sometime Sheriff of London and Middlesex. He was a master builder whose company laid out local streets, housing estates and shops for the predominantly Irish workforce escaping famine in their native country. On the right is the red-brick Docklands Community Centre, home of The Island History Trust, where there are over 5,000 photographs of life in the docks through the ages.

Shortly after the Community Centre, as the road rises, turn off the path at the pedestrian crossing and go immediately left through a black iron gate. Head up the rise, climbing steps to the uppermost path, which is the route of a railway that once carried the rope-laying machines of the nearby

Globe Rope Works (1881–1971). Beneath the path on both sides are allotments, pigsties and paddocks, for you are walking above the 35-acre (14-hectare) Mudchute City Farm. At the end of the path turn left, passing a playgroup, into Pier Street. Turn right, cross Manchester Road and continue past residential estates named after such nautical luminaries as single-handed round-the-world sailors Frances Chichester (1901–72) and Chay Blyth (b. 1940). Turn left at Seyssel Street and follow signs to Riverside Walkway until you reach the river at Saunders Ness (Ness is derived from the French *nez* for 'nose', referring to the nose-shaped lie of the land).

The name Saunders appears on a 16th-century map of the Isle of Dogs and the road itself follows the line of an ancient track, which topped the wide tidal embankment of earth, wood and stones. The track – a kind of early version of the Isle of Dogs Westferry/Manchester ring road, but with an uninterrupted view of the Greenwich and Blackwall Reaches – once followed the entire loop of the Isle of Dogs from Limehouse to Blackwall. The bank was constructed to protect the area, which was known until 1800 as Poplar Marsh or Stepney Marsh, from flooding at high tide; the land inside the loop was drained with open ditches and turned into pasture. Here are views of Blackwall Reach, the Greenwich peninsula and Greenwich itself. Dominant is the Greenwich Power Station, which dwarfs the white Gothic almshouses that sit beside it.

As part of his development of the area, Cubitt divided the foreshore here into lots where shipbuilders, repair works and timber wharves set up business at the river's edge, backed by brick fields and cement works. The embankment was raised and straightened so that wharves could be built and ships could be moored alongside. Over a hundred years later, in the 1960s and 1970s, industries were closing down and were eventually replaced with the housing estates you see today.

Soon the Riverside Walkway circuits Newcastle Drawdock, a low-tide unloading spot for barges. The path continues on the far side back to Island Gardens.

VICTORIAN GIANTS: ROYAL DOCKS-NORTH WOOLWICH

Summary: A thrilling introduction to the Victorian docks, where today great sheets of water lie among partly developed wasteland. Wide skies, the dramatic outlines of towering cranes, gleaming new bridge designs and planes taking off from City Airport to business centres throughout Europe all combine to create a sense of an exciting future. Wellingtons aren't necessary, but be prepared for bracing breezes as this area is vast, flat and very exposed.

Start:	Royal Victoria DLR Station
Finish:	North Woolwich Railway Station
Distance:	4½ miles (7.5km)
Refreshments:	Supermarket and wine bar at Britannia Village; otherwise take your own!

A Riverside Revolution

The walk begins at Royal Victoria DLR Station. From the station, go straight ahead for the dockside, passing a brightly coloured pumping station on your right. Turn left and walk alongside the dock, looking back to see the Millennium Dome and the distant new Docklands. Pass beneath giant industrial sculptures that were once working cranes and now stride the length of the quay like surreal giant insects.

When the Royal Victoria Dock opened in 1855, covering 80 acres (32 hectares), it was the biggest area of impounded water in the world, almost half the size again of the two (import and export) West India Docks combined, and with double the capacity. Though further away from the commercial and trading hub of the City, distance was no longer an issue, for the Age of Rail had arrived and it was railway tycoons, rather than merchants, who put up the money. At around 35 feet (10.5m) deep, Victoria, and its companion dock, Albert, were more than 9 feet (2.75m) deeper than West India Docks and could accommodate the new iron steam ships that were being built. In the second half of the 19th century, steam ships had the engines, speed, reliability and increased cargo space to compete with sailing

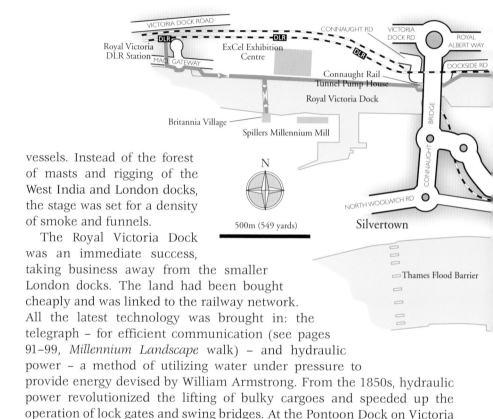

vessels. Instead of the forest
of masts and rigging of the
West India and London docks,
the stage was set for a density
of smoke and funnels.

The Royal Victoria Dock
was an immediate success,
taking business away from the smaller
London docks. The land had been bought
cheaply and was linked to the railway network.
All the latest technology was brought in: the
telegraph – for efficient communication (see pages
91–99, *Millennium Landscape* walk) – and hydraulic
power – a method of utilizing water under pressure to
provide energy devised by William Armstrong. From the 1850s, hydraulic
power revolutionized the lifting of bulky cargoes and speeded up the
operation of lock gates and swing bridges. At the Pontoon Dock on Victoria
Dock's south side (across the water from where you are walking), ships
could, for the first time, be lifted out of the water by hydraulic machinery
and onto pontoons for repair.

Today, the long perspective of the quay is largely deserted, but when
the dock was in business it was packed with piles of pallets and crates and
the air was filled with the din of working gantries, rumbling wheels, the
hiss and roar of steam and engine, blaring ships' horns and workers'
shouts. Bulky cargo ships and towering hulls of passenger liners were
berthed in continuous lines where now a handful of sailing dinghies dart
like water insects, dwarfed by the vast rectangle of water.

The Royal Docks specialized in handling goods that were lower in value
but bulkier than the wines, spirits and luxury cargoes of the older
docklands closer to the City, although Victoria usurped St Katharine Docks'

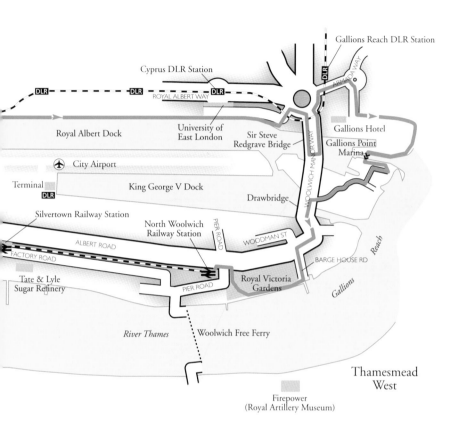

Gallions Reach DLR Station

Cyprus DLR Station

DLR · · · DLR · · · DLR · · · DLR
ROYAL ALBERT WAY

Royal Albert Dock

University of
East London

Sir Steve
Redgrave Bridge

Gallions Hotel

Gallions Point
Marina

✈ City Airport

Terminal
DLR

King George V Dock

Drawbridge

Silvertown Railway Station

North Woolwich
Railway Station

PIER ROAD

ALBERT ROAD

WOODMAN ST

FACTORY ROAD

BARGE HOUSE RD

Tate & Lyle
Sugar Refinery

PIER ROAD

Royal Victoria
Gardens

Gallions

Reach

WOOLWICH MANOR WAY

ARMADA WAY

River Thames

Woolwich Free Ferry

Thamesmead
West

Firepower
(Royal Artillery Museum)

monopoly of the tobacco trade. Wheat, barley, oats, peas, seeds and timber
came from America and Russia and – once refrigerated holds had been
introduced – there were cargoes of meat from Australia and New Zealand.

Old Meets New

Pass hotel and office developments in various stages of completion until
you reach a huge square fronting the ExCel Exhibition Centre. Set back
from the dockside here are a few remaining yellow-brick warehouses from
c. 1855. More in keeping with the new-look docks, however, is the
suspension footbridge ahead, which at first doesn't seem to connect to
the ground, although it does by lift. It's worth taking a brief detour along
the footbridge for spectacular views up and down the dock or to stock up
at the little supermarket in the 'urban village' of Britannia. There's little
other opportunity for refreshment along the dockside, though moored
nearby is a yacht that has been converted into a hotel.

Look across the water for glimpses of the steel helmets of the Thames Flood Barrier and, dominating the opposite quay, the huge reinforced granaries of Spillers Millennium Mill, which dates from the 1930s. Victoria Dock housed Britain's largest conglomeration of flour mills, each with its own silos and pneumatic elevators to lift grain into the granaries before being downloaded to barges to be transported to other mills. A century after Victoria Dock was completed, both the dock and its neighbouring extensions enjoyed a greater volume of business than ever before, but with the advent of containerization and the demand for even bigger ships the Victorian docks gradually became redundant during the 1970s and were closed in 1981.

At the end of Victoria Dock you reach Connaught Passage, which connected to the 1880 dock extension known as Albert Dock. Some extension! The new dock was enormous: 1¼ miles (2.1km) long, with 3 miles (5km) of quays. This was the first major dock to have electricity, enabling through-the-night unloading. The little yellow-brick building is Connaught Rail Tunnel Pump House: the railway line was diverted through a tunnel beneath the passage so that ships would not have to wait for overland trains to pass. On a warm day, the swing bridge is a favourite spot – despite danger notices – for local children to dive from.

To the right is your first view of City Airport and on the opposite quay is a sugar refinery: Tate & Lyle were big in Silvertown, the area south of the docks, from the 1880s. City Airport runways now run between Royal Albert Dock and the last of the royal docks to be built, King George V, which was completed in 1921. George V was smaller, but geared up to take the biggest ships afloat at the time, such as the P&O passenger liner *Mauretania*. The airport ran its first flights in 1987 and now handles 1.6 million passengers a year.

Rebirth in Prospect

Building works in progress might hamper a direct quayside route to the University of East London, whose colourful, tilted windmill shapes lie ahead. Once on the campus, there's a path straight through the middle, but you may have to go left around the building sites and right at Cyprus DLR Station to find it. The water here has been marked out as an international rowing course, although an oarsman friend once remarked, with feeling, that it was far too windy and exposed.

Opposite: A suspension footbridge, with fantastic views up and down Royal Victoria Dock, will take you across to the Britannia Village development where you can purchase refreshments for the onward walk.

Where the university exit road meets a roundabout, turn right (signposted North Woolwich) across Sir Steve Redgrave Bridge – fittingly named after the five-times Olympic Gold-winning oarsman. The bridge separates Albert Dock from its entrance basin. Though this stretch is busy with road traffic, there are superb views: along the dock side of the bridge is a panorama of sheets of water reaching towards the new Docklands, planes taking off and landing along the strip of City Airport and the cluster of cheerful university buildings. Return along the basin side of the bridge, from where you can see out to Gallions Reach, named after the Venetian galleys that were once a feature of the waterscape. Rising alone from a wasteland is the turreted and gabled red-brick Gallions Hotel, built to accommodate passengers of the P&O liners. Haunted though it looks now, plans for the 2012 Olympic and Paralympic Games aim to transform this area and the lower reaches of the River Lea into a city park and a regenerated far East End of London.

At the roundabout, take the Gallions Reach DLR Station exit and carry on to the next roundabout. Take the third exit here and, just before the barrier gate to a site entrance, turn left down an unmarked path. There's a fence at the end of it, but it's easy to bypass to go directly onto a neglected Thames-side path. Turn right and follow the river's upstream sweeps until you reach Gallions Point Marina. Cross over the locks at the marina entrance and turn left to Gallions Point jetty to see the river's changed character. Industry and town have petered out, at least for a while, and the low wooded landscape is perhaps not too different from the one that greeted the Romans. Spare a thought for the 640 people who drowned after a day trip downriver along this reach, about a mile (1.6km) downstream from Woolwich when, in 1868, the *Princess Alice* pleasure steamer collided with the iron collier *Bywell Castle* and sank.

Turn back and take the main service road leading left, back towards the royal docks. Rejoin Woolwich Manor Way just past Sir Steve Redgrave Bridge and turn left to follow the road as it curves across the drawbridge over the King George V Dock entrance and then round to the right. Take the second turning left down Barge House Road. At the end, go up the ramp and down the slipway to the Thames Path and turn right. The route is grubby, grey and concrete and skirts an abandoned drawdock, but very soon the Royal Victoria Gardens on your right bring green relief. On the far shore is Firepower, the Royal Artillery Museum – formerly the Royal Arsenal, where the manufacture of ammunition and gunpowder began in 1696; there, too, is the site of Woolwich Dockyard, now Thamesmead West estate (see pages 91–99, *Millennium Landscape* walk). At the end of the gardens, turn right to go into them and on to the exit gate on the left. Turn left and follow the road round to North Woolwich Station.

ROYAL FAVOURITES: GREENWICH CIRCULAR

Summary: Rarely for this book, there's some hillwalking – over the rollercoasters of Greenwich Park for sweeping views of the Thames and Docklands. Greenwich, with its glorious royal past, also evokes key moments in navigation, exploration and naval history, with insights en route into the achievements of Sir Francis Drake, Captain James Cook and John Harrison, whose chronometer enabled accurate navigation at sea.

Start & Finish:	Maze Hill Railway Station
Distance:	3 miles (5km)
Refreshments:	Greenwich town centre; Trafalgar Tavern; the Yacht

Turn right from Maze Hill Station and left and right to cross into Greenwich Park by the gate near the corner. Take the path that follows the walled boundary of the park. Look obliquely right to see steps leading up the hill (at about the point where there is a door set into the wall on your left) and head for these. The steps take you to the summit of 'Belov'd of thousands, One Tree Hill', apparently one of Elizabeth I's (1533–1603) favourite spots. The quotation comes from *The London Chronicle* of 1784 and is carved into the semicircle of benches that commands a view of docklands old and new.

Retrace your steps from the hill and take the first fork right. At the intersection, just past a splendid avenue of sweet chestnuts marching down the steep grassy slopes to your left (topped by one with a trunk resembling twisted ship's cables), take the right-hand downhill path (signed Queen Elizabeth Oak) and keep straight ahead at the next intersection. The oak, whose remains lie beside a young upstart of a sapling, in fact predates Elizabeth I and is believed to have been big and hollow enough to have been used as a lock-up in the 12th century. It finally died in the 1800s, but over the following decades was propped up by a framework of ivy until it finally collapsed in 1991.

Most of the trees in Greenwich Park were planted by King Charles II (1630–85), and there are Spanish chestnuts, oaks, limes and plane trees that date from his time.

Greenwich's Role in Naval History

From Queen Elizabeth Oak head uphill towards the Old Royal Observatory, which was founded in 1675 by Charles II for 'the finding out of the longitude of places for perfecting navigation and astronomy' and designed by Sir Christopher Wren. The hilltop statue near the observatory is of General James Wolfe (1727–59), a Greenwich man who led the English against the French up the Heights of Abraham in Quebec and died a hero's death there. The victory gave Britain possession of the former French colony.

The observatory, a planetarium and a museum of navigational instruments and timepieces are incorporated into Flamsteed House, which was named after the first Astronomer Royal. Correct your watch as you stand at zero longitude – the boundary between the eastern and western hemispheres and the point from which the world's time is calculated – in the courtyard of Flamsteed House. A prize was offered for the person who could come up with a reliable means of calculating longitude, so that time and distance calculations could establish exact position at sea. The solution was John Harrison's fourth chronometer, which was tested by explorer Captain James Cook on his second Pacific voyage of discovery and became his 'never-failing guide' to navigation. If you are at Flamsteed House at 1pm you can watch the ball on the observatory's weathervane drop, which was a visual time-check for mariners on the Thames to set their chronometers by.

From the museum, turn left down a steep path that leads to the cross-park route of The Avenue. Continue on to exit the park into King William Walk and take the second left along Nelson Road. Cross the main Greenwich High Road to go down a narrow path to the right of St Alfege Church. Alfege was the 29th Archbishop of Canterbury, who was captured by Viking raiders and murdered on the site of this church in 1012. The present-day building was designed by Nicholas Hawksmoor (1661–1736), one-time clerk to Sir Christopher Wren and later a distinguished architect in his own right, and dates from 1714. It is also where General Wolfe was buried and General Gordon of Khartoum (1833–85) was baptized.

At the point where the path corners left, turn right into the graveyard-cum-park and head immediately right via tombstones to emerge into Bardsley Lane. Go left to the end of the lane and left again along the main road over Deptford Creek. After the bridge, cross the road to turn right and follow the creek among housing developments. Deptford – meaning 'deep ford' – is the mouth of one of London's almost-lost rivers, the

Opposite: The 19th-century tea clipper Cutty Sark, *which now sits in a dry dock in Greenwich, was once the pride of British shipping due to its speed and success in the race to bring tea back to England from the Far East.*

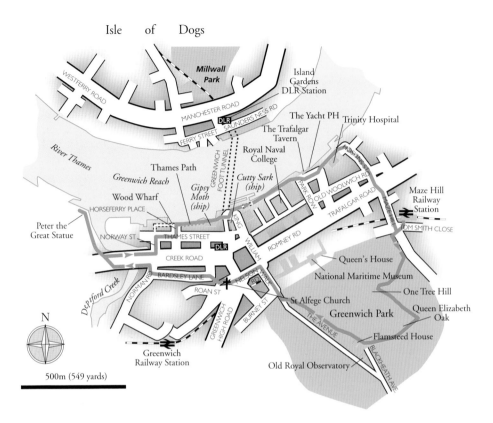

Ravensbourne. Once the source of power for numerous corn mills, the riverside is now largely inaccessible and functions as a storm-relief sewer.

The Navy-building Town

Waterside residential development has opened up a short stretch of riverside walkway, which is cut short by the Royal Naval Yard further along. It was along this stretch of river that Henry VIII (1491–1547) founded the royal dockyard that established Deptford as a major shipping centre for over 300 years. Deptford was long known as the 'navy-building town', but over the centuries the docks were used less and less until they finally closed in 1869. They were replaced by a cattle market, though part of the area today, at Convoy's Wharf, is once again a working dock, with a 'ro-ro' (roll-on, roll-off with minimum red tape) facility for paper imports.

The Elizabethan adventurer Francis Drake (1540–96) moored the *Golden Hinde* here in 1579, after his pioneering circumnavigation voyage that laid the foundations for the East India trade (see pages 48–57, *Georgian Dock*

Boom walk). Drake was knighted on board by Queen Elizabeth I. The Queen ordered that the ship be kept at Deptford 'as a memorial of national honour and imperial enterprise'. It eventually disintegrated, but a working replica can be seen near Southwark Bridge (see pages 100–110, *Wharves and Warehouses* walk). It was at Deptford, too, that the ship *Resolution* was fitted out for Captain Cook's remarkable voyages of the 1770s, during which he ventured on untried routes round the world, twice crossing the Antarctic Circle, and discovered South Georgia and the South Sandwich Islands in the southern Atlantic.

Continue towards the Thames and turn left. On your left is an impressive statue, donated by Russia, of Peter the Great (1672–1725) with a dwarf. Such was the reputation of England's sea power that Peter, Tzar of all the Russias, visited Deptford for a few months in 1698 to study shipbuilding. His behaviour during his trip was rather less than great: he stayed at the nearby house of diarist John Evelyn (1620–76) and partied every night. Evelyn returned to find broken furniture, grease and ink stains on the walls, torn bedlinen and bullet holes in paintings that had been used for target practice; the once carefully tended lawn looked like a battlefield.

Retrace your steps to the bridge over Deptford Creek and turn left into Norway Street and left again into Horseferry Place. At Wood Wharf turn right along the Thames Path. Ahead you will soon see the domed entrance to the Greenwich Foot Tunnel, which opened in 1902 after being built to Sir Alexander Binnie's designs and replaced the horse-ferry service that had been running since 1676. The tunnel provided a handy cut-through to the Isle of Dogs docks for Greenwich labourers. It emerges via a twin entrance in Island Gardens.

Clippers and Yachts

Your eye is drawn to the spire-like masts of the tea clipper *Cutty Sark* lying in dry dock ahead; it's easy to pass by the ocean-going yacht *Gipsy Moth IV*, which is berthed on the left and dwarfed by the clipper. This was the boat in which 65-year-old Francis Chichester sailed single-handedly to Australia and back in 1966–7. The challenge was to see if a modern yacht could match the times achieved by the 19th-century racing clippers, such as the *Cutty Sark*. It fell some way short but, nevertheless, Chichester's was the fastest voyage ever made in a small vessel at that time: he covered 29,630 miles (47,482km) in 226 days. Francis was knighted by Queen Elizabeth II (b. 1926), with the same sword with which Elizabeth I had knighted Francis Drake at Deptford. *Gipsy Moth IV* is no longer open to the public and, indeed, if funds become available, it may be completely refitted and restored to take part in the 2005 Blue Water round-the-world rally.

Clippers, such as the *Cutty Sark*, were so called because they clipped time off given schedules. They were also known as windjammers or ocean-going 'racehorses' as they competed against each other to rush cargoes of tea from India and China. Even after the advent of steam power, products that did not deteriorate with travel, such as tea, continued to be carried in sailing ships. Different companies competed against each other to break the record for the shortest journeys, but speed was also a top priority for more practical reasons: the first consignment of the yearly crop of tea fetched high prices on the London market and won a bonus for the crew.

In 1885 the *Cutty Sark* sailed from Australia to England via Cape Horn in 72 days, breaking the record for the fastest voyage. She was the last of the windjammers to carry tea from India and China and wool from Australia in the 19th century. Even as she was launched in 1869, the newly opened Suez Canal was threatening her future: steamships could cut through the canal, shortening the journey between Europe and India by 7,000 miles (11,690km). The clippers still had to sail round Africa, vulnerable to the vagaries of the wind. The *Cutty Sark* was rigged to squeeze every possible advantage out of the wind. More than 11 miles (18.4km) of ropes controlled 32,000 square feet (2,973 sq.m) of canvas sail – equivalent to the area of 11 tennis courts. The ship's figurehead is Nonnie the Witch, a character from Robert Burns's poem 'Tam O'Shanter', dressed in her nightshirt-like 'cutty sark' or short blouse. There are many figureheads on display below deck.

Nautical Memorabilia
Given the nautical theme of this walk, it is worth visiting the National Maritime Museum, where you can immerse yourself in Britain's maritime history from Tudor times to the present. Sail through maps and manuscripts, ship models and paraphernalia, valuable memorabilia of naval heroes and explorers such as Captain Cook and Admiral Lord Nelson and gaze at portraits galore. To visit the museum, go inland from the *Cutty Sark* and cut left through the main avenue of the former Royal Naval College. Turn right and cross the main road to the next block of impressive buildings back from the river – the Queen's House, a perfectly balanced gem of Palladian architecture by Inigo Jones (1573–1652), which was completed in 1638 and is flanked by the museum. To rejoin the route walk through the central avenue of the former Royal Naval College buildings and turn left at the end towards the Trafalgar Tavern.

The Palace of Placentia
Alternatively, on the far side of the *Cutty Sark*, simply continue along the riverside path and pass beneath the long façade of the Royal Naval College.

This was the site of the splendid Royal Palace of Placentia that was loved by King Henry VIII and his daughter Elizabeth. It was where King Henry married Catherine of Aragon in 1509, and where their daughter, later Mary Tudor, was born, as was Elizabeth, daughter of Henry's next queen, Anne Boleyn. The Palace was wrecked during the civil wars (1639–60) and fell into ruin. The joint Protestant monarchs William and Mary, who reigned from 1689, decided to found a hospital for seamen on the site. They hired three of the greatest architects of all time: Sir Christopher Wren, Nicholas Hawksmoor and Sir John Vanbrugh (1664–1726).

Tzar Peter the Great commented that the finished building – great blocks of Baroque architecture separated by courtyards to preserve the river views – was wasted on 'worn-out seamen' and more fitted to royalty. Queen Mary had hoped that wounded, sick or aged seamen would 'live safely moored' in the hospital, but the institution was damned in the 18th century for being harshly run; as one Captain Baillie commented in 1771, 'columns, colonnades and friezes ill accord with bully beef and sour beer mixed with water'. The punishment for the slightest misdemeanour was for the offender to wear his uniform inside out, exposing the bright yellow lining. The end of the Napoleonic Wars (1803–15) brought a decline in wounded sailors, and the hospital was finally closed in 1869. It was taken over by the Admiralty as a naval college and since the Navy left in 1998 it has been let by a charitable trust.

Whitebait Dinners

The riverside path leads straight to the magnificent Trafalgar Tavern, built in 1837, whose balconies and bow windows were inspired by the galleries of Elizabethan man-o'-war ships. The pub was fashionable with 19th-century politicians and literary figures enticed by its 'whitebait dinners' served with iced champagne. One such was Charles Dickens, who set the wedding feast in *Our Mutual Friend* here. In the high whitebait season (from April to August), the river below would be busy with fishermen from Lambeth, Rotherhithe and Greenwich in their rigged clinker-built 'peterboats'.

Turn left down a flagstoned alleyway at the back of the Trafalgar past the Yacht pub, whose walls are hung with photographs of famous yachts, and a terrace of neat Georgian and modern houses, back to the riverside. On the right is the quirky Gothic Trinity Hospital, which has been home to a succession of local elderly retired gentlemen since 1617. On the wall opposite are engraved marks, which record exceptionally high tides of the past.

When you reach a wall set with charming bas-relief tiles that tell *A Thames Tale*, turn right to the cross the Old Woolwich Road and Trafalgar Road and head up Maze Hill to return to the railway station.

SURREY SIDE UP: ROTHERHITHE PENINSULA

Summary: In the beginning, the Rotherhithe peninsula was low-lying and waterlogged. Rotherhithe itself was a fishing village and the rest of the land was of little use for farming and settlement. By the 18th century, shipyards lined much of the waterfront, and by the 19th century almost the entire peninsula was taken up with back-to-back dock basins. Today, much of what used to be known as the Surrey Commercial Docks has been reclaimed by urban planners. The result is a delightful and accessible mix, with enough remnants of former docklands to conjure up an impressively industrious past, some unexpected wilderness and a network of waterside paths.

Start and Finish: Rotherhithe Underground Station
Distance: 4 miles (6.7km)
Refreshments: Pubs in Rotherhithe Street and at Greenland Dock; shopping mall at Canada Water/Surrey Quays

Route of the Pilgrim Fathers

Turn left out of Rotherhithe Underground Station and left again into Railway Avenue, passing Marc Brunel's 1800 Thames Tunnel engine house on your left (see pages 100–110, *Wharves and Warehouses* walk). Turn right into Rotherhithe Street, opposite Tunnel Wharf, and turn left at a little Thames-side garden at Cumberland Wharf onto the Thames Path. There, overlooking the reach of the Thames from which the *Mayflower* sailed in 1620 with many Rotherhithe pilgrims on board, is a statue of a Pilgrim Father and his lad by Peter McLean. Let your imagination sail and steam through the centuries, picturing in turn Elizabethan galleons, top heavy and billowing of sail, streamlined clippers bound for the Far East and Australia, steamer packets taking passengers to Gravesend, Ramsgate, Dover, Boulogne and Ostend and coasters bringing in cargo from Ipswich, Yarmouth and Hull.

The stretch by the river is brief; all too soon, you are forced to return to Rotherhithe Street, but there's drama ahead in the form of the red-girdered

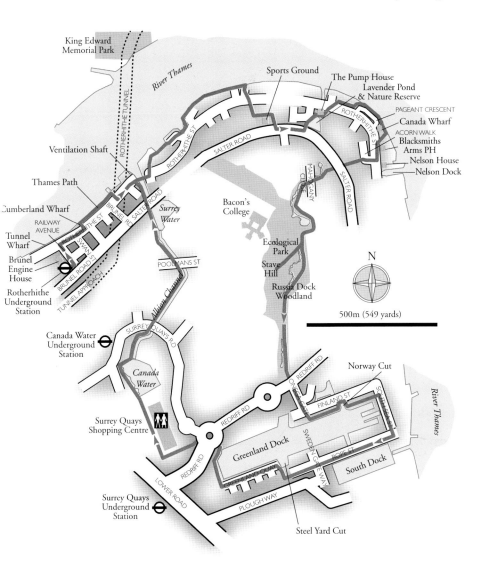

bridge over the outlet of the Surrey Water dock. Before you cross it, look left to see the ornate circular red-brick building. Its twin is across the river in the King Edward Memorial Park (see pages 48–57, *Georgian Dock Boom* walk), and they are, in fact, ventilation shafts for the Rotherhithe Tunnel, completed in 1908 (not to be confused with Marc Brunel's Thames Tunnel, which runs a little further upstream). The Rotherhithe Tunnel provides a handy road route to the new Docklands, but the footpath is not recommended because of the traffic noise and fumes. The tunnel's entrance, beneath a steel arch, is in Lower Road, Rotherhithe, and is marked by a section of the 'shield', a 30-foot-diameter (10-m) cylinder which, powered by hydraulic jacks, was used to inch through the bedrock beneath the Thames.

Rounding the Loop

Cross the bridge and turn left at the big pub to walk past block after block of riverside apartments and around or across inlets, until you reach a dead-end; turn right, back onto Rotherhithe Street opposite Lavender House, cross the road and turn left, then head right down the path signed Lavender Pond and Nature Park. Take the immediate left turn uphill to skirt two sides of a sports ground, then turn left into Salter Road. After a few yards, just before a pond, turn left, passing a small but beautiful nature reserve and the Pump House, which was created by the Port of London Authority in 1930 to maintain the water level in the local docks.

Go straight across the road, through a courtyard separating blocks of riverside residences, turn right and you will be struck by a close-up of Canary Wharf and the Isle of Dogs, for you have rounded a big loop in the Thames. Pass by an obelisk and continue to the yellow-brick wall of a six-storey warehouse. This is the tastefully converted, late 19th to early 20th-century Canada Wharf. Return to the road and turn left past the Blacksmiths Arms and the elegant mid-18th-century Nelson House. Nelson Dock was a pioneering shipyard, producing wooden sailing ships and later composite hulls of timber overlaying iron frames.

Opposite Nelson House take the path marked Acorn Walk. Kink immediately left and immediately right uphill. Fork right and follow the path to an underpass with mosaic pictures. We are heading towards Russia Dock Woodland, which, as its name suggests, is a wildlife park created from a former dock. Following the closure of the Surrey Docks in 1970, 423 of the peninsula's 460 acres (186 hectares) of dockland were filled in. Continue straight up, ignoring paths to the right and left until the second footbridge, where you turn sharp left, signposted Ecological Park and Bacon's College, to pass ponds bordered by rich woodland. Follow the second pond round to the right and just before the next bridge take a clear

Opposite: As the evening sun slowly sets, Canary Wharf's skyscrapers, as seen from across the Thames at Surrey Water on the Rotherhithe peninsula, glow bronze. Here, the landscape has changed dramatically over the last 20 years.

right turn and another right which leads to Stave Hill. This symmetrical, man-made hill, which resembles a prehistoric burial mound, has splendid views over the sea of trees to the Isle of Dogs; in the opposite direction, pick out the London Eye and Tower Bridge.

A Graphic History Lesson

Resist going down the enticing poplar- and lime-lined avenue that leads from the hill; instead, retrace your steps back down the path you came up and turn right at the first junction. Turn right again at the next T-junction, then immediately left. The part-cobbled path has mooring bollards and sections of rail for the travelling cranes of yesteryear, and borders a grassy basin, once a rectangle of water thick with working boats. If you've completely lost your sense of direction by now, look down at the end of this stretch to see the points of the compass set into the ground, with its exciting and graphic evocation of trade and commerce past.

Cargoes of softwood and other timber travelled 1,203 miles (2,009km) from Leningrad in the Baltic Sea; tar, oil and tallow were imported from Gdansk, Poland, and wheat and dairy produce came 3,135 miles (5,235km) across the Atlantic from Montreal, Canada. The dock basins that handled the goods took the names of the countries or regions they traded with: Baltic (completed in 1809), Canada (1876) and Quebec (1926). In an attempt to combat stiff competition from the other London docks and the railways, the individual dock companies south of the river amalgamated to form the Surrey Commercial Dock Company in 1864. As with London's other docks, the Surrey docks were enclosed and secure, with access strictly limited to official workers. They were also custom-built to transfer goods from ship to quay and warehouse much more efficiently than was possible at riverside berths.

As you walk the length of the quay the contrast between industrial past and parkland present is dramatic. Turn right to an underpass, which is actually the bed of the canal lock link between Greenland and Russia Docks, and you'll see the other end of what was the Surrey Canal on the far side of Greenland Dock, which you are just about to meet. The canal was constructed between 1802 and 1805, when it ran through countryside to link with the Thames at Rotherhithe, but it was swallowed up by the Greenland Dock enlargement of the 1890s.

The Last of the Surrey Commercial Docks

Beyond the underpass, follow the left-hand path to the north quay of Greenland Dock, the largest surviving remnant of Surrey Commercial Docks. Its watery rectangle is as it was following the 1890s enlargement of the original Howland Wet Dock. This was one of London's earliest enclosed commercial docks, built between 1696 and 1699 and capable of holding 120 sailing ships. It became the main berthing for Arctic whalers and was soon renamed Greenland Dock. The original dock predated the Georgian docks on the north bank of the Thames by a century, but it was not allowed to handle dutiable cargoes.

In the 19th century, Greenland Dock went on to become the main UK port for timber from Scandinavia and the Baltic countries; the Surrey Docks as a whole were the world's biggest timber importers. Great towers of stacked planks and logs rose in blocks along the quay, separated by what were known as the 'roadways', which also provided some sort of fire break. For more than a century, Canadian grain was also a staple import in Greenland Dock and in the 1930s more than 2 million tons of tinned food, bacon, cheese, butter and fruit from North America were imported every year. The closure of Greenland Dock accompanied the general demise of the Surrey Commercial Docks in 1970; the basins just weren't deep enough for the vessels that were now transporting timber and grain.

The apartment blocks that surround Greenland Dock are arguably no more attractive than the transit sheds, warehouses and giant cold stores that lined the quays before the Second World War (most of these were destroyed in the Blitz, sounding the death knell for the North American foodstuffs business), but at least today the dockside is open to the public.

The Ravages of War

Turn left to follow the northern edge of Greenland Dock, passing over the Norway Cut swing bridge and a huddle of old barges, tugs and steamers. Turn right at the end of the dock to go along South Sea Street; over to the left are the iron bridge and lock that mark the dock's gateway to the Thames. Carry straight on, through the housing estate, and turn right at South Dock.

All along the Thames estuary, the river and docklands were a primary target for the German air force. The Surrey Docks suffered more damage than any other British dock area. In September 1940, the entire 350,000-ton stock of timber was destroyed by fire in a single night; the flames could be seen 30 miles (50km) away. But the London docks kept going and contributed massively to the war effort. Here at South Dock – and at Russia Dock, too – concrete blocks each weighing 3,375 tons were constructed at breakneck speed to make the 2-mile (3.3-km) floating Mulberry harbour for the D-Day landings in Normandy in 1944. The finished harbour enclosed an area 70 times larger than Greenland Dock. Look to the right for Steel Yard Cut into Greenland Dock. Because the lock had been

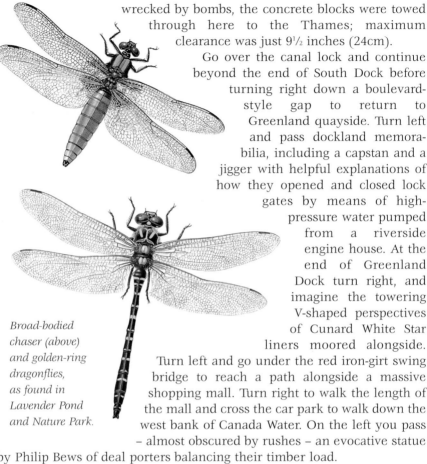

wrecked by bombs, the concrete blocks were towed through here to the Thames; maximum clearance was just 9½ inches (24cm).

Go over the canal lock and continue beyond the end of South Dock before turning right down a boulevard-style gap to return to Greenland quayside. Turn left and pass dockland memorabilia, including a capstan and a jigger with helpful explanations of how they opened and closed lock gates by means of high-pressure water pumped from a riverside engine house. At the end of Greenland Dock turn right, and imagine the towering V-shaped perspectives of Cunard White Star liners moored alongside.

Broad-bodied chaser (above) and golden-ring dragonflies, as found in Lavender Pond and Nature Park.

Turn left and go under the red iron-girt swing bridge to reach a path alongside a massive shopping mall. Turn right to walk the length of the mall and cross the car park to walk down the west bank of Canada Water. On the left you pass – almost obscured by rushes – an evocative statue by Philip Bews of deal porters balancing their timber load.

Near the end of the road, look left to the clock tower of the late Victorian dockmaster's house; in dramatic contrast is the airy glass structure of Canada Water Underground Station opposite. Turn right at the junction, then right again down a footpath over a corner of Canada Water. Just before the footbridge, turn left down Albion Channel. This is London's answer to Amsterdam, a narrow waterway that ribbons its way calmly through residential developments. Follow it all the way, past Surrey Water, until the red swing bridge over Rotherhithe Street that you encountered at the beginning of the walk and turn left to retrace your steps to the station.

MILLENNIUM LANDSCAPE: GREENWICH EAST–WOOLWICH

Summary: The destination is Woolwich, home of the Thames Flood Barrier and one of the first royal dockyards, via the bleak but thrilling Greenwich Peninsula. En route, you will pass working wharves that are significant in industrial history, the redundant but still sensational Millennium Dome and some interesting examples of contemporary landscape architecture and environmental planning. It's an exciting walk, as the ever-broadening Thames changes in character as it prepares to meet the sea; this landscape has been reclaimed from despair more than once and is again on a positive course.

Start:	Maze Hill Railway Station
Finish:	Woolwich Dockyard Railway Station
Distance:	5 miles (8.3km)
Refreshments:	Pubs at Ballast Quay, Greenwich; Anchor and Hope pub, Woolwich

Turn right from Maze Hill Railway Station, cross Trafalgar Road right and turn left into Lassell Street. Greenwich Power Station, the titanic building with a tower at each corner, which makes it resemble an upturned table, once provided power for the London tram system and now serves London Underground. Head to the riverside path and turn right into cobbled Ballast Quay, with the Cutty Sark pub, whose building dates from at least the beginning of the 18th century, and a row of later 18th-century houses. The ballast handled from this quay was made up of river dredgings and sand and gravel from Blackheath, just inland from Greenwich. Ballast was big business: it was a neat and profitable way of disposing of the spoil from dock excavation, and provided stability for vessels emptied of their cargo. Look out for the symmetrical lines of the 1855 harbourmaster's office on the right, from which the quay's business was monitored together with

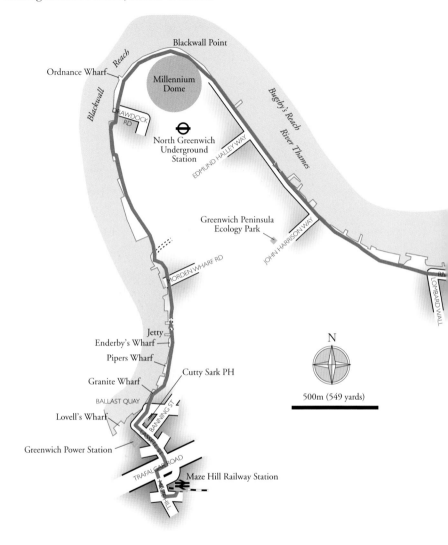

collier traffic that plied the river between Limehouse Stairs and Blackwall Point at the tip of the Greenwich Peninsula.

Working Wharves

Turn left from the quay onto the Thames Path (signposted Greenwich Peninsula West and Thames Barrier) for the working-wharf stretch of the walk. This gives an idea of what the whole area must have been like a few decades ago. First comes Lovell's Wharf, which was a working wharf until

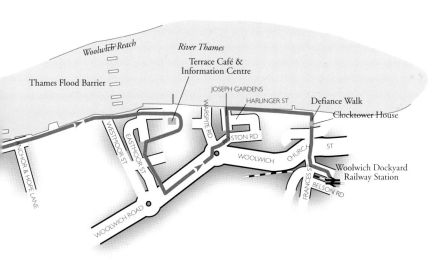

the 1980s, when it was handling 118,000 tons of cargo of non-ferrous metals. Next comes Granite Wharf, where barges unloaded great blocks of stone, including Portland and Purbeck stone from Dorset, to be dressed and worked for such fitting monuments as Admiralty Arch, the London base for British sea lords.

You may not hear the clink of hammers on metal and the flash and roar of welding equipment that you associate with a working boatyard, but the high fence at Piper's Wharf encloses a boiler house and floating dock, where lighters and workhouse barges that ease the loads of bigger ships are still brought for repair. For years in the early 20th century, Piper's barges dominated Thames Barge Races.

Just beyond the slipway, a rusting hulk and a tangle of aquatic plants are backed by the dazzle of the buildings of new Docklands across the broad reach of water.

The Enderby Legacy
You will next reach Enderby's Wharf, where technological progress is captured in information panels. The wharf's history and name stem from

the Enderby family, who by 1790 were managing a fleet of whaling boats from this quay. As for many merchant adventurers, exploration and the mapping of new areas were natural extensions of their business. Charles Enderby was a founding member of the Royal Geographical Society; there is an Enderby Land in Antarctica, and several parts of the continent are named after captains in the Enderby fleet. For Herman Melville (1818–91), writing in his whaling novel *Moby Dick* (1851), the family ranked in importance alongside 'the united royal houses of the Tudors and Bourbons in point of real historical interest'. The white house on the right, now offices, was the power base of the Enderby family; they worked from an office in the glass-domed octagonal room.

The Enderbys diversified into rope-making in the 1830s, and later specializations on this site were appropriately cable-loading machinery and telegraph cable production. The wharf's greatest moment in history came in 1865, when the transatlantic cable that made the first telegraph connection between Europe and America was loaded onto the only ship large enough to carry it, Isambard Kingdom Brunel's *Great Eastern* (see pages 65–70, *Bulk Cargo* walk). When the cable was laid on the ocean bed between Ireland and Newfoundland, five words a minute could be transmitted electronically (if the words were short!). Displayed on the quay is a 'repeater' of the type that is placed at 35-mile (58.5-km) intervals along the line to boost the signal; today, enough words to fill a million copies of the Bible are transmitted every second. Hi-tech communication continues in Greenwich today: in 1980 the first submarine optical cable was developed by a Greenwich-based company.

Just north of Enderby's Wharf is Bay Wharf, which enjoyed its moment of glory in the Second World War when barges for the invasion of France were constructed there.

A Dramatic Landscape

The ebb and flow of industries, both living and dead, are evoked in the dramatic buildings – and sometimes distinctive odours – of such businesses as waste disposal, starch and sugar refineries, towering grain silos and a power station, followed by a small marina. A cluster of willow trees brings relief from all the hard work. Shortly after, follow the path round to a fenced diversion, signposted for the Millennium Dome. Pass the old wooden wharves that have been creatively preserved: one is planted

Opposite: The distinctive futuristic metal domes of the Thames Flood Barrier cover essential electro-hydraulic operating systems that power large gates which can be closed to prevent severe flooding when a surge tide threatens London.

with mosses and stonecrops; another, once the scene of jostling cargo boats and coasters with all the accompanying human activity, is now a wildlife reserve on stilts. Plants such as sea aster, sea buckthorn, teasel and evening primrose have been transplanted from similarly exposed areas downriver.

Nearing the tip of the peninsula sits Ordnance Wharf, site of the first industrial development on this reclaimed marshland in the 1690s. Guns, rifles and thousands of barrels of gunpowder were distributed from here, but the site was closed on safety grounds in the 1760s. We follow the river's course round Blackwall Point, past a propeller-like sign that stands astride the Greenwich Meridian (see pages 77–83, *Royal Favourites* walk) and mountains of gravel waiting to be carried on overhead chutes to fill the holds of moored ships. Take a second look at what appears to be another boat moored alongside: it is, in fact, a sculpture – *Slice of Reality* by Richard Wilson.

To the Dome and Beyond

You are now encircling the impressive but disused Millennium Dome, which, when it was built on the site of an old gas station, was the world's largest dome, with a circumference of over half a mile (835m) and a 95,650 sq.yd (80,000sq.m) roof. The remarkable fabric covering, which stretches over a network of steel hawsers supported by 12 masts, is just ⅛ inch (1mm) thick.

The tip of Greenwich Peninsula is a prime spot for watching wildfowl, particularly species such as oystercatcher, shelduck, dunlin, redshank, cormorant, snipe and teal, as they commute along the river highway between feeding grounds. The tidal marshes on the foreshore are rich habitats for shrimps, crabs and other invertebrates. The river is relatively quiet and clean compared with days gone by: from the 17th century onwards the Blackwall Shipyard across the river was churning out ships from East Indiamen to tea clippers, including the first steam ship (the *City of Edinboro*) in 1821 and naval frigates. Ballast barges, small tankers and coal carriers plied between the estuary and strings of busy wharves, their cargoes dispatched to Greenwich peninsula's brick and cement factories. Far beneath your feet runs the Blackwall Tunnel – a vital commuting facility for Kent-side labourers working in the Georgian and Victorian docks of the Isle of Dogs and Canning Town.

As you circuit the point and take in the wildlife on tidal terraces, reed bed, salt-marsh and foreshore, Blackwall Reach gives way to Bugsby's Reach. Bugsby, it is conjectured, is a common American name, so the reach may have been named after a New World sailor or pirate. Bugsby's

Hole, a tidal mudflat nearby, was the point where the bodies of pirates hanged at Execution Dock (see pages 58–64, *Georgian Docks Revisited* walk) on the far bank, were suspended in iron cages until three tides had washed over them.

An Air of Desolation

Now, as the riverside path opens up on the eastern stretch of the peninsula, there's a dramatic change of mood as the Canary Wharf cityscape is left behind and the river begins to anticipate its meeting with the sea. Imagine its origins as a miasmic, mosquito-ridden salt-marsh until, in the 17th century, Dutch engineers built walls and embankments on the river to curb flood tides. Their efforts, together with a 1625 drainage programme, made the salt-marsh habitable for the first time. Osiers and reeds were grown commercially for basket-making, and wildfowling and fishing were the main livelihoods. The 19th and 20th centuries brought a host of industrial sites that no one else would tolerate in their back yard: oil refineries, gas works, chemical plants and power stations, leaving a legacy of badly contaminated land. For much of the 20th century, this was the unhealthiest part of London, and local residents and workers had the highest level of industry-related illness in the country. Today, it is a landscape in the throes of death and creation simultaneously.

Inland, desolate wasteland and abandoned works are interrupted by Millennium Village high-rises, while the riverside borderland is a triumph-in-waiting of ecologically sensitive landscaping. Beaches, salt-marsh terraces and mudflats are being protected and improved under the direction of the Environment Agency, and banks are stabilized naturally with waterside plants and reed beds. The broad perspective of the walkway is punctuated with striking sculptures, including a steely polar sundial, and Antony Gormley's *Quantum Cloud*, a spiky steel net condensing into a 30-foot (10-m) human body, which is one of the UK's tallest sculptures.

Keeping the Sea at Bay

Soon, you pass the wetland wildlife reserve of Greenwich Peninsula Ecology Park, which washes the feet of yellow, red, orange and blue high-rise apartments. It's worth taking a right turn to walk through the reserve before returning left to the Thames Path, signposted for the Thames Flood Barrier, which is soon in sight, striding across the river. If bad weather strikes, you may, like many a skipper of the past, be forced to anchor and hope that things improve at the well-named *Anchor and Hope* pub. The pub is also one of several to claim to be where 18th-century printmaker William

Hogarth (1697–1764) sketched out his illustrated moral tale of the ill-fated idle apprentice, who ended up being hanged for highway robbery. Pass Riverside Gardens, where traces of a Roman fort and an Iron Age settlement have been discovered, and continue to the Thames Barrier, which, for a while at least, is intended to prevent a combination of north wind and surge tide that could cause devastating floods.

Much of London lies on a broad flood plain, 2 to 3 miles (3.3 to 5km) wide; parts of areas such as Rotherhithe and the Isle of Dogs are reclaimed marshland and actually lie below high-tide level. In 1242, flood water stretched 6 miles (10km) from Lambeth to beyond Elephant and Castle; in 1579 fish were seen in the flood water that lay in the Great Hall at Westminster Palace; and in 1953 over 300 people were drowned in floods along the Thames Estuary and the east coast. The threat of future floods increases all the time, as the south of England is gradually sinking, ice caps are melting and the water level is rising. In the worst-case scenario, a combination of northerly winds and surge tides could flood London's underground system and seriously contaminate the water supply; thousands of people would have to be evacuated and the capital would be paralyzed. The Thames Flood Barrier's shelf-life expires in 2030. Until then, when a surge tide threatens, the 10 giant gates, each one around 65 feet (20m) high, are rotated from their normal position on the river bed to form a steel wall facing downriver to stem the incoming wall of water. Inside the gleaming stainless-steel helmets are the electro-hydraulic operating systems.

Sea aster

Henry VIII's Woolwich

Go up steps and round to the right to walk under the flood barrier; continue until steps lead up to the Terrace Café and Information Centre. At the time of writing, the next part of the route is an 'interim path' directing us inland. Go behind the café towards the Learning Centre and turn right along the road, following the walls of a red-brick factory-cum-warehouse. At the junction – with a 'noted stout house' (now an animal welfare clinic) on the right – go straight across to walk along a cycle path through a little park planted with silver birches. At the main Woolwich Road, turn left following the 'interim footpath' sign to a pub overlooking a roundabout. Take the second left to go past warehouses dominated on your right by a big chimney, the site of the former Boiler Works and Iron Foundry.

Turn left into what was once part of Woolwich Dockyard, founded in 1513 by King Henry VIII, but is now a housing estate. Woolwich probably started off as a harbour and market for wool: this is what the Anglo-Saxon name signifies, just as Lambeth was possibly a 'lamb wharf', for animals being transported across the river from the grazing fields of Essex. Henry changed all that by deciding to build his new dockyards at Woolwich and Deptford instead of Portsmouth. They were closer to the armouries and labour supply of London and to the king's favourite palace at Greenwich. The establishment of the Royal Laboratory, later the Royal Arsenal, half a mile or so downstream in 1695 was even more convenient for complementary arms supplies, and the dockyard held its own for the next couple of centuries. In the 19th century, despite having the first plant for repairing ships' steam engines in a naval dockyard, it failed to keep up with technological advances, and eventually closed in 1869. Woolwich was also a garrison town, home of the Royal Artillery, but this too has now gone.

Go straight across a break in the housing estate through an unlocked iron gate to the riverside. Opposite is the massive Tate & Lyle sugar refiners' complex. Turn right and continue along the riverside, up and over an iron folly of a footbridge and, when you reach the cannons, turn right up the steps. The route via Defiance Walk passes the 18th-century Clocktower House on the right. This was the former base of the Admiral-Superintendent of the dockyard, whose job was to make sure that Admiralty instructions were carried out. Exit through the old dockyard gates and cross the road to Woolwich Dockyard Railway Station, which you see ahead to the left.

WHARVES AND WAREHOUSES: ROTHERHITHE–TOWER OF LONDON

Summary: This walk reveals a cross-section of London's history as a port, starting at the former fishing village of Rotherhithe and passing through the slums and warehouses of Victorian times to the sites of the original Roman port of Londinium and of medieval trade. You get a sense of London's changing fortunes and the impact of foreign invasion through the ages and learn about lighters, Legal Quays and the role of warehouses in international trade. It is a boom-and-bust story, with periods of flourishing trade followed by decay and despair and, at the beginning of the third millennium, a new life and a new look.

Start:	Rotherhithe Underground Station
Finish:	Tower Hill Underground and DLR Station
Distance:	3 miles (5km)
Refreshments:	St Mary Church Street, Rotherhithe; Hay's Galleria, Butlers Wharf

Pioneering Engineering

From Rotherhithe Station turn left and immediately left again into Railway Avenue. The yellow-brick building on the left is the Brunel Engine House, which provided steam power for the construction of the revolutionary Thames Tunnel. This was built in 1843 by Marc Isambard Brunel, helped by his promising son, Isambard Kingdom. An exhibition inside the tunnel tells the story of its building. It was one of the first tunnels to be built under water and used a pioneering 80-ton tunnelling shield, which not only prevented the soft river-bed clays from caving in, but was divided into working cells from which the navvies could hack away at the rock face. Nevertheless, the tunnel claimed several lives through flooding and the leaking of dangerous gases and took 17 years to build. It was one of London's must-see sights for visiting dignitaries and within 24 hours of opening around 50,000 people had walked through it. Stalls were set up in recesses in the tunnel walls, but the damp and gloomy route was always unpleasant. In 1869 the East London Railway Company bought the tunnel and created a railway link between Rotherhithe and Wapping, making this one of the oldest sections of underground railway in the world.

Religious Associations

From the engine house, head towards the river, turn left along Rotherhithe Street and go straight across Tunnel Road, keeping to the right of Victorian warehouses on the corner. Shortly on the right is the Mayflower Inn, named after the ship that was chartered in Rotherhithe by the Pilgrim Fathers to go to America in 1620. Many of the Pilgrims – a separatist Protestant sect escaping persecution – came from this area.

Opposite the Mayflower Inn turn left into the cobbled street bordered by warehouses and then right into St Mary Church Street. The elegant church was designed by John James, an associate of the rather more famous Sir Christopher Wren, and completed in 1715. The style of the church's structural features and the skill involved in creating them indicate that the work was perhaps done by local shipwrights. The fact that the church is built on a plinth to protect it against flooding reminds us of the threat posed by the tidal Thames. Inside the church are wood carvings by master craftsman Grinling Gibbons (1648–1721). Nautical relics include an oak table and two bishop's chairs made of oak recycled from the warship *Téméraire*, which played a key part in the Battle of Trafalgar in 1815 against the French emperor Napoleon. There is also a commemorative plaque to Christopher Jones, captain of the *Mayflower*, who was buried here in 1622. The ill-fated Prince Lee Boo, prince of an Indonesian tribe, is commemorated here too. He was brought to England in 1783 by the captain of the packet ship *Antelope*. Lee Boo was a novelty in London and became something of a celebrity, but 13 months after his arrival he died of smallpox.

Opposite the church, note the two painted plaster figures of schoolchildren above the door of St Mary Rotherhithe Free School, which was founded by local mariner Peter Hills in 1613 (though this building dates from the early 18th century). Opposite is Hope Wharf, which includes an early 19th-century granary with a hipped roof. Legal Quays, where customs officials checked incoming goods on which duty could be charged, were introduced in the Pool of London, downstream of London Bridge, in 1558 (see pages 149–158, *Bridging the Thames* walk). With increasing trade, however, they became overloaded with work, and many lower-value imported goods came to be handled at these sufferance wharves on the south bank and at St Katharine Docks. Next door is the village watch house and fire-engine house, dating from 1821.

Local History

Continue along St Mary Church Street to The Ship pub, then turn sharp right and follow the trunk-like curve of Elephant Lane towards the river at King's Stairs Gardens, passing the solitary office of Braithwaite and Dean, a firm of Thames lightermen. Like many of the barges that sailed the tidal Thames, lighters – vessels that 'lightened' the loads of bigger cargo ships – had flat, boxlike hulls that could hold a lot of cargo and 'take the ground' at low tide. Initially, they were rowed or steered, moving with the flow of tides and currents, but later they were towed by tugs. Lighters also evolved into sailing barges with large square sails. In the 18th century, small sails were added fore and aft to improve efficiency when sailing against the wind.

Turn left to go undercover along the riverside path, which is flanked by a shiny red-brick wall. On the right is the Angel pub, which, despite its run-down exterior, is full of character inside. It was founded in the 15th century by the monks of Bermondsey Priory to refresh passing pilgrims, but soon became a haunt of smugglers and pirates and a place where unfortunate drinkers might be press-ganged into crewing ships. Navigator and explorer Captain James Cook spent many hours here planning his trip to Australia.

This stretch of river bank was settled by Neolithic and Bronze Age people between two and three thousand years ago, and traces of a 3,500-year-old timber causeway that once led across the marshy Rotherhithe peninsula have been discovered. Just past the Angel there's a group of sculptures by Diane Gorvin entitled *Dr Salter's Daydream* and a plaque that describes the life of this remarkable man. Dr Salter and his wife dedicated their lives to the poor of Bermondsey, a commitment that led indirectly to the death of their daughter. The sculpture depicts Salter in happier times, waving to his daughter; the family cat sits on the sea wall.

Look to the left now and imagine the moated mansion that stood here 700 years ago. In the 14th and 15th centuries, the riverside lands of the south-east were scattered with the homes of many wealthy landowners and ecclesiastical dignitaries, and this was one of King Edward III's residences. Today, the course of the moat and a crumbling wall are all you can see, but there's a helpful plan of how the mansion looked. Continue along Bermondsey Wall East until a cluster of trees announces your arrival at Cherry Gardens. The view from here was the setting for British artist J.M.W. Turner's engraving of the warship *Téméraire* on her final journey to a Rotherhithe breaker's yard.

Opposite: Gleaming in the sunshine at high water, but thick with mud at low tide, St Saviour's Dock is all that's left of the Neckinger River; the former grain, pea and spice warehouses that flank it are now apartments and offices.

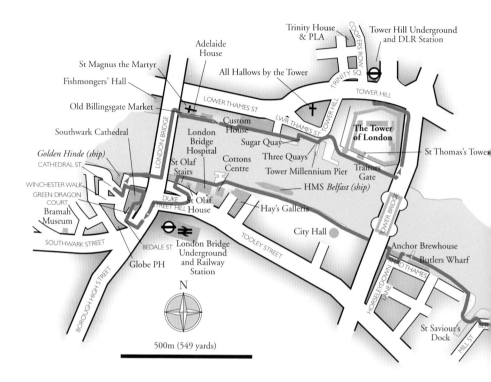

Follow the Thames Path until you break away from the river by turning left into Fountain Green Square, with the Old Justice pub ahead, right along Bermondsey Wall East and left down Loftie Street. As you turn right into Chambers Street, you are dwarfed by the severe and impenetrable giant blocks of Chambers Wharf cold stores, which were built in the 1930s. At the end, turn right to join Bermondsey Wall West and, when the road turns sharply left, go straight ahead along a narrow path that goes under the corrugated orange and white building that is China Wharf (designed by Piers Gough and completed in 1988). Turn left to rejoin the Thames Path and go over the new suspension footbridge that crosses St Saviour's Dock, where the river slaps brown-grey and dense with mud. St Saviour's Dock was once the mouth of another lost river, the Neckinger; the tidal inlet to which it was reduced was the site of grain, pea and spice mills in the 19th century.

A Dickensian Scene

We are deep in Victorian warehouse territory here. Despite the opening of the big Georgian docks across the river, many riverside wharves on the south bank survived, dealing with trade from around Britain's coast and with duty-paid foreign cargo, which was transferred from the docked ocean-going ships by lighters. To deal with this cargo – swollen by the booming international trade of the first half of the 19th century – merchant companies invested in more and more warehousing, much of it on the south bank. Look out for surviving features, such as wall-mounted crane jibs by the loading doors. Inside the warehouses were winches, capstans, treadwheels and hydraulic jiggers to transfer the cargo. The riverside here went under the names of Folly Ditch and Jacob's Island and was surrounded by stinking millstream ditches. It was overcrowded, poor, dirty, black with smoke and, according to Charles Dickens, populated by 'unemployed labourers... ballast-heavers, coal-whippers, brazen women,

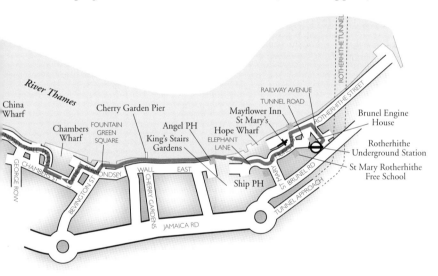

ragged children, and the raff and refuse of the river'. It was here that he wrote of the villain Bill Sikes falling to his death from a warehouse ruin in *Oliver Twist* (1837).

Across the bridge is Shad Thames, with its river frontage, and Butlers Wharf, which was once the largest concentration of Victorian warehouses on the Thames, extending 131 yards (120m) inland. Now there are café terraces, expensive apartments and offices, dramatic iron sculptures that evoke ships' anchors and propellers and a useful location map detailing what you can see across the river. In the 1850s, the combined effects of a relaxation in customs duties on many goods and the repeal of the Corn Laws brought about a boom in trade. Six- to eight-storey warehouses began to replace the old riverside wharves, some of which contained their own silos for the bulk storage of grain, while breweries had their own granaries in which to store barley.

Exotic Imports

Towards the end of the run of restaurants, turn left off the Thames Path to join the cobbled street of Shad Thames, a relic of 19th-century industry, emerging opposite the 1891–2 Cardamom Building. The exotic names of buildings and streets – Cuba, Jamaica, Cinnamon – recall the cargoes once stored here. For an insight into the history of these key imports and their impact on trade, travel and society, visit the Bramah Tea and Coffee Museum. Look back at high-level walkways used to transfer goods from wharves to warehouses. At the end of Shad Thames, just before you pass under Tower Bridge, look right to the Anchor Brewhouse, where the Scotsman John Courage brewed his first 51 barrels of beer in 1789. The present building, which once was a combined boiler house, brewery and malt mill, was rebuilt in the 1890s; the brewery closed in 1981. Opposite is Horseleydown Lane, where the brewery's dray horses rested up.

Tower Bridge, completed in 1894, was designed by Sir Horace Jones, who was also the architect of Old Billingsgate Market, which you can see on the opposite bank of the river. The bridge's towers complement those of the Tower of London nearby. In its heyday, the bridge opened to let river traffic through up to 50 times each day; now it's about 900 times in a whole year.

Your route is now paved with smooth blue-grey limestone brick, courtesy of Foster and Partners, the architects responsible for the tilting glass hemisphere of City Hall. This is the headquarters of the Greater London Authority and office of the Mayor of London. Its shape and tilt expose the minimum surface area to the sun and stepped floors shade those beneath. Instead of expensive air conditioning, the building is cooled by a water cooling system that is fed by underground water drawn up through boreholes. Panoramic views are to be had from the top-floor walkway. Looking upriver towards London Bridge you can see another Foster construction: the 2003 Swiss Re building, popularly known (owing to its shape) as 'the gherkin'.

Ships Ancient and Modern

The way ahead is obvious, past the battleship grey of HMS *Belfast*, a battle cruiser built for speed and manoeuvrability and the last big armoured ship in Britain's Royal Navy. She was launched in 1938, saw active service in the Second World War and was saved from the scrapyard to come under the jurisdiction of the Imperial War Museum. A striking comparison is to be had with the replica of the 16th-century *Golden Hinde* further along this route. Next comes the magnificent shopping mall of Hay's Galleria. Alexander Hay built up his business empire on this site from 1651. The warehouses of 1856–7 were built in the fashionable Italianate style. The Hay's Wharf Company was famed for the fleet of tea clippers that brought tea from India to its warehouses, but it also pioneered cold storage and brought shipments of butter from New Zealand. Peep inside for the spectacle of the high arched roofs and the giant iron sculpture *The Navigators* by David Kemp (1987), an eccentric and delightful confection of nautical instruments contained in the shape of a ship's bow.

Inside the glass-fronted atrium of the Cottons Centre (Cotton's Wharf that was) members of the public can sit beside tropical plants and fountains. Now serviced offices, the original warehouses were where a bale of jute notoriously caught fire in 1861. The resulting conflagration, the Tooley Street Fire, fuelled by cotton, spices, rags and oil, raged for two weeks and consumed many warehouses, including the buildings on the western side of Hay's Dock (now Hay's Galleria), which had been completed just four years before. Outside the Cottons Centre are helpful plans pinpointing what you can see across the river. From this spot, too, are the best views of London Bridge Hospital, which took over the 19th-century warehouses with their Doric-style pilasters and sweeping arches, and the Art Deco St Olaf House. Norseman King Olaf joined forces with the English King Ethelred to recapture the City of London from the Vikings in 1014.

Continue along the path past these two buildings and turn immediately left down St Olaf Stairs. Turn right and cross to London Bridge Station. From here, cross Borough High Street into Bedale Street opposite London Bridge Underground Station and then right just before The Globe pub into Green Dragon Court. This is the site of London's first ever recorded vegetable market, dating from before the 11th century. The tradition continues with the bustling Saturday market of today. Turn right from the market to go round the back of Southwark Cathedral and bear left at the fork to visit the replica of the *Golden Hinde*. The replica has circumnavigated Britain and toured North American ports, and is an exact reconstruction of the square rigger that carried the Elizabethan adventurer Sir Francis Drake around the world between 1577 and 1580; the average height of the crew was just 5 feet 4 inches (1.65m). The ship measures a mere 120 feet (37m) in length, compared with HMS *Belfast*'s 613 feet (188m), and weighs 305 tons, compared with *Belfast*'s 91,000 tons. From the ship, retrace your steps and turn sharp left at the fork to pass in front of the cathedral. Just downstream from here are traces of the timber bridge built in AD 1000 by the Saxons (see pages 149–158, *Bridging the Thames* walk).

The Roman City

Go up the steps just before the pedestrian tunnel and cross London Bridge. The north bank at this point was the centre of the Roman port of Londinium. Soon after their AD 43 invasion, the Romans developed their new port around a gravel stretch on the otherwise silty shore, and built the first timber London Bridge, about 160 foot (50m) in span, across the shallowest crossing place, downstream of the present bridge. Londinium became an administrative centre for the northern Roman Empire and was the principal port for goods coming in from other parts of the Empire, such as olive oil from North Africa, wine from Italy and pottery from France; grain, cattle and hides, gold, silver, iron, pewter, hunting dogs, oysters and slaves were exported. When the Empire crumbled and the Romans left, trade declined slowly but surely, the port silted up and the wooden bridge collapsed. By AD 500, the once-thriving port town had been abandoned.

The building on the left below the bridge is Fishmongers' Hall (1831–5), designed by 28-year-old Henry Roberts on the site of a 2nd-century Roman quay and, since the 14th century, a meeting place for fishmongers. Cross the road here and go down steps to the Three Quays riverside path and head downstream over the footbridge. Pass the white building with star motifs, which is Adelaide House. When it was built between 1921 and 1925, it was London's tallest commercial building and the first to have a mini-golf course on its roof! Behind the riverside buildings is the church of St Magnus the Martyr, where a well-seasoned wooden remnant of one of the Roman jetties can be seen. Near here, too, were Roman baths overlooking the river; some well-preserved remains have been excavated.

The Famous Fish Market

The fish connections continue: look at the lamp posts along this stretch of the river and at the weathervane on the next building you come to. This is the Old Billingsgate Market, which operated on this site from the early Middle Ages until 1982, when business moved east to the North Quay of the West India Docks on the Isle of Dogs. Billingsgate Quay was one of London's oldest and busiest docks. Traditionally, it had long been a landing place for fresh produce, as well as timber, coal and corn, although a 1698 Act of Parliament established it as London's principal fish market. Citrus fruit and onions from Spain and salt were also landed there and the old wharf was the main landing for coal; the now demolished Coal Exchange was situated a little further along. By the 16th century, Billingsgate had superseded London's other busy quay of Queenhithe (see page 156, *Bridging the Thames* walk), just a little upstream, in importance. It had the advantage of being downstream of London Bridge, having a deep, recessed harbour and proximity to the City. Billingsgate developed its own peculiarities of language, its own characters and dress and gained notoriety. 'Fish fags', 'Billingsgates' and 'fish-wives' were all terms inspired by the gin-toting, pipe-smoking, tough, loud and foul-mouthed women of Billingsgate, who were also renowned for their bare-knuckle fighting.

The Billingsgate building you see today dates from 1875 and was designed by the Tower Bridge architect Sir Horace Jones. It comprised a wood and brick market hall, a gallery from which cured fish was sold and a vaulted basement for shellfish, shops and warehouses. Trading there ended in 1982, when the market moved to new premises further east. The old fish market building was refurbished in 1989 by Richard Rogers.

Policing the River

The path here is flanked by blue railings above a stretch of the river where, from at least the 13th century, boats drew up to have their cargo assessed for import duty. The present Custom House building on your left, with its magnificently long façade, dates only from 1812–17, however. It was the administrative heart of port business, controlling the registration of ships, import and export duties, policing and smuggling. Ships' captains came ashore to register their goods in the Long Room. Customs officials known as 'tide waiters' boarded incoming vessels downriver at Gravesend and accompanied them to their moorings; then 'landing waiters' took over and weighed, measured and assessed the cargoes. In the mid-16th century, 20 ocean-going vessels a week had to be processed and this one quay could not cope, so Legal Quays were set up along the north bank between London Bridge and the Tower of London to spread the load. Each quay specialized in particular goods, which are recalled in the names given to parts of this walk; Sugar Quay, though, is named after the Tate & Lyle sugar processing company that built its headquarters here in the 1970s.

The Medieval City

We are now at the heart of the medieval port of London. The early Saxons had based their port of Lundenwic (see pages 149–158, *Bridging the Thames* walk) in the area that now lies beneath Covent Garden and the Strand. From the late 9th century, the port's focus was back downriver, where the Romans had originally built Londinium and the first London Bridge. Between 1176 and 1209, the first stone London Bridge was constructed. The Norman Conquest opened up cross-Channel business opportunities, and trade – especially in fine-quality English wool – flourished. By the mid-14th century, London was Britain's largest port and the city's population was sustained by imports from around Britain and Europe –

wheat and barley from upriver country towns, such as Henley, and fish from Rye and Great Yarmouth. Shipwrights, coopers, fishmongers, mercers (dealers in cloth) and other craftsmen and traders banded together in associations called guilds to protect their interests.

Look across the river here to the high curving arch of Hay's Galleria: in medieval times, the view would have been dominated by granaries and breweries. You have to go round the Tower Millennium Pier by turning left. Ahead, up the hill, you can see the grey porticoed pile – adorned by a swarthy statue of the sea god Poseidon – of the Port of London Authority (PLA) buildings. The PLA was set up in 1909 to take over responsibility for the enclosed docks and the management of the river below Teddington Lock. Next to it is Trinity House, the 20th-century headquarters of a company formed by royal charter in 1514 to manage pilots, buoys and beacons in the Thames Estuary and to keep the waterways clear of silt. Trinity House was also granted exclusive rights to sell ballast dredged from the river, which was used to stabilize boats that had discharged their cargo.

The Tower of London

Now turn right towards the entrance to the Tower of London and right at the red postboxes set into the wall to walk along the riverside defences. Many of the towers doubled as watergates, which allowed access and could be shut to keep the dangerous high-tide water under control. The main watergate, beneath St Thomas's Tower, is now called the Traitors Gate. Edward I had apartments on the top floor in the 13th century and the lower part later housed a tide mill that operated the Tower's water supply. The heart of the Tower was built over 900 years ago by William the Conqueror (*c.* 1027–87) to impress and intimidate both the English natives he had just conquered and the invading Danes. It has served through the centuries as a prison for enemies of the State, an armoury, the royal mint, a stronghold for the royal family in times of danger and a storage place for Crown treasures and records. The wharf was a landing place for royalty and foreign dignitaries, as well as for captives facing imprisonment or execution. Since the reign of Henry VIII, guns have been fired from here to mark national celebrations.

At the end of the tower frontage, turn left up some steps onto Tower Bridge and walk inland to the end of the Victorian iron railings, then left down some steps to the landscaped area north of the Tower. Ahead you can see the copper spire of All Hallows by the Tower. Turn right at the roundabout round the medieval postern or gate tower – the eastern entrance to the medieval city – through the underpass and straight up the steps to Tower Hill Underground and DLR Station.

THE WORKING WANDLE: RIVER THAMES–MERTON ABBEY MILLS

Summary: The River Wandle is the most interesting of the London Thames tributaries, because it offers a unique record of industrial history, which started long before the Industrial Revolution. Much of the Wandle survives above ground and you can follow it on foot along most of its course. The northern stretch, from the Thames to Merton Abbey Mills, is where most of the industry was focused. You can link to the following walk (pages 118–24, *The Rural Wandle* walk) to follow the river to its source.

Start:	Wandsworth Town Railway Station
Finish:	Colliers Wood Underground Station
Distance:	4½ miles (7.5km)
Refreshments:	Various pubs, cafés and shops in Wandsworth and Earlsfield; Merton Abbey Mills

The Wandle's drop over its course, from the flanks of the North Downs to the Thames, and its strong, even flow have made it useless for navigation, but great for water power, and it was one of the best rivers in England for driving mills. In addition, the Wandle was linked by the great artery of the Thames to the ever-hungry markets of London, and it neither flooded nor froze over in winter.

Harnessing the Tides

From Wandsworth Town Station, turn right and cross Swandon Way to turn first right into Smugglers Way. Turn left onto The Causeway, which was once the road to the village square over the marshy delta of the Wandle. Before this area was drained and built up, it was a plain laced with the Wandle's many streams. From medieval times until the late 19th century, a nearby mill harnessed energy from the rise and fall of the tides and willow shoots or osiers were cut for basket-making and thatching. Just to the east – towards the centre of London – ran a canal, which linked the

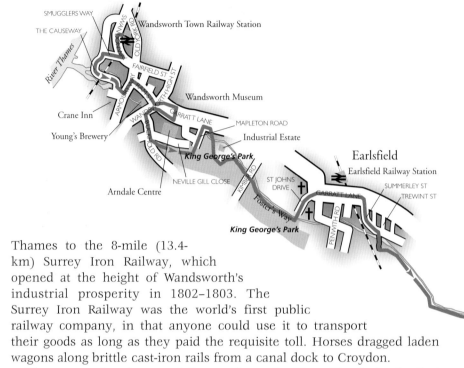

Thames to the 8-mile (13.4-km) Surrey Iron Railway, which opened at the height of Wandsworth's industrial prosperity in 1802–1803. The Surrey Iron Railway was the world's first public railway company, in that anyone could use it to transport their goods as long as they paid the requisite toll. Horses dragged laden wagons along brittle cast-iron rails from a canal dock to Croydon.

There were already several flour mills on the River Wandle by the first millennium. Gradually, many other industries and settlements were established and the Wandle valley became a thriving commercial centre, reaching the peak of its prosperity in the early 19th century. As local historian Dorian Gerhold records, 'few other parishes in the country had such a range of industries as Wandsworth'; in 1805, the Wandle was described as the hardest worked river in the world. The mills were working the river to the limit, using its energy to power industries as diverse as lavender and leather processing and the production of beer, gunpowder, chocolate, textiles and paper.

Tracing the Wandle's Route

Cross the Wandle and turn left (signposted for the town centre) along a brick path on the west bank of the river and then on a boardwalk past a landscaped area with some hopeful willows enclosed by black railings. When you reach the Crane Inn, cross the main road (Armoury Way) and turn left then right into Ram Street. This is not a pretty sight today, but in

Wandsworth's agricultural prehistory it was the site of Ram Field. Later the street formed the border of the Surrey Iron Railway. Sleepers from the old railway can be seen in the yard of Young's Brewery on the next corner on the right. Commercial brewing is recorded as having taken place here since 1576, which makes this the longest-running brewery site in Britain. Young's Brewery is open to the public and inside you can see 19th-century beam engines, historic brewing equipment and, in the stables, heavy dray horses. Cross Wandsworth High Street into Garratt Lane to visit the Wandsworth Museum in the Old Courthouse.

The river disappears beneath the large and dreary Arndale Centre, which was intended to be the largest shopping mall in Europe when it was completed in 1971 and which we have to circuit. From the museum, cross Garratt Lane and return, turning right, to the High Street. Turn left and left again into Buckhold Road (signposted King George's Park and the Wandle Trail). A few yards along, past Neville Gill Close, turn left through the wrought-iron gateway into the park. The park, created in 1921, took the place of open fields and a rubbish dump. Pass a magnificent willow by the pond on the left and follow the path to the rose garden. Turn left where there's a children's playground on the right, following the sign for Wandle Trail and Kimber Road, and exit the park at Mapleton Road.

A dyeworks operated near here from *c.* 1720 to 1830 and may have been established long before then. Many textile-finishing processes were to take advantage of the Wandle's energy and abundant clean water supply. The level, low ground of what is now King George's Park was ideal for creating the shallow ditches that were used for bleaching calico. The meadows were divided into strips of grassy banks and ditches and the calico was spread over the grass to be bleached by the sun, a process that took about a month in fine weather. From the mid-16th century, immigrants from the Low Countries and Huguenot refugees escaping

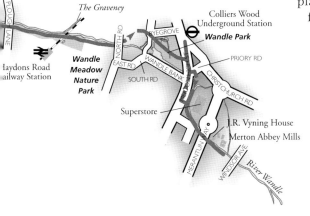

500m (549 yards)

The Graveney

Colliers Wood
Underground Station

Wandle Park

PRIORY RD

Haydons Road
Railway Station

**Wandle
Meadow
Nature
Park**

NORTH RD

EAST RD

SOUTH RD

RYEGROVE

WANDLE BANK

CHRISTCHURCH RD

Superstore

MERANTUN WAY

WINDSOR AVE

J.R. Vyning House
Merton Abbey Mills

River Wandle

religious persecution in France were attracted by the Wandle's natural resources, and the skills and technology the immigrants brought with them were fundamental to the area's industrial growth.

At the road junction, turn right and you will see the Wandle emerge and flow beneath the 1902 bridge. Turn right down a brick path across the river again and back to the park. Turn left past the sports field, towards the steps, and follow the park perimeter. An industrial estate echoes the Wandle's past, but once again the river disappears. Go straight across Kimber Road and across Foster's Way, still among the playing fields of King George's Park. Where another block of factories ahead bars access to the river, turn left across the bridge and go through the housing estate to St Johns Drive. There

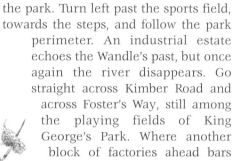

Kingfisher

follows an unfortunate but brief stretch along busy Garratt Lane through Earlsfield. Once one of many rural estate villages, Earlsfield is a prime example of the encroachment of London suburbia into the countryside, which was particularly rampant after the opening of the railway station in 1884.

A Legacy of Pollution

Pass the station on your left, turn right down Summerley Street and follow the road round to the left until you meet the river once more near the site – at the end of Trewint Street – of one of the gunpowder mills that made Wandsworth England's second largest supplier of gunpowder in the late 17th century. Mill power was used to compress the potent mixture of saltpetre, charcoal and sulphur.

Cross the bridge and turn left down to the riverside path. Here, in the shadow of another industrial estate, this rural stretch may help you imagine the river as a once-famed trout stream, in spite of the odd shopping trolley and sundry rubbish. Pollution finally killed off the fish in the 19th century,

Opposite: This house, which encapsulates the Arts and Crafts Movement's ideals of simplicity and function, overlooks the River Wandle at Merton Abbey Mills, which was an important focus of the Movement's activity.

but today there are once again a few hopeful fishermen, and riverside plants and birds find peace from the never-ending roar of suburban traffic. Pass beneath the pylons, past a power station and cross Plough Lane. Turn left then right to continue on the riverside trail on the opposite bank. Soon, under the railway bridge, the river meets its only significant tributary, the Graveney, which flows, mainly below ground, from Tooting.

At the junction, ignore the signpost, which has had its signs turned so as to be useless. Turn right to a pond (where another vandalized sign recounts the life cycle of the frog) and turn left across the gravel path over Wandle Meadow and a nature reserve. Look out for rectangular indentations in the ground – traces of the former sewage works. This is a cared-for spot, where the locals have regular clean-up days and where kingfishers are known to ply the route from further upstream.

Messrs Nelson and Morris

The path goes through a tunnel beneath North Road, then heads diagonally over the next open space to join a small residential road. There's a former waterworks on the right; keep to the left of it and pass a terrace of modern houses. Cross the road to a gateway in the brick wall into Wandle Park. Follow any of the paths leading south through the park towards the fountain in the far left-hand corner. This pocket of natural beauty, where the Wandle has been nurtured into streams and wildlife ponds, was opened in 1907 and is now under the auspices of the National Trust. It was formerly the grounds of Wandle Bank House, one-time home of a friend and neighbour of Admiral Lord Nelson. The fountain is a relic from the grounds; pause a while to read the apt inscription at its base, a quotation from Matthew Arnold's 'Lines Written in Kensington Gardens', before you emerge to the 'city's jar' of Merton High Street.

Turn right and cross the road to the business estate opposite. It's hard to imagine that there were once commercial watercress beds here! Go to the right behind the first block of commercial buildings and turn left at the Pickle Ditch noticeboard (with restoration and nature notes) to follow the river. The hypermarket lies over the old site of Morris & Co., founded in 1881 by William Morris (1834–96), pioneer of the Arts and Crafts Movement and probably the most influential designer of the late 19th century. Morris abhorred the drudgery of mass production and wanted to recapture the simplicity and creativity of medieval craftsmanship. Many of his distinctive chintzes, tapestries and carpets were produced on this site, together with stained glass, and sold through the Regent Street department store Liberty, who printed their own famous fabrics at nearby Merton Abbey Mills.

Turn right across the footbridge at the hypermarket entrance and immediately left along a pretty wooded stretch of the Wandle. This area caught the attention of Emma, Lady Hamilton (*c.* 1765–1815), mistress of Admiral Lord Nelson (1758–1805): in 1801 she bought the adjacent Merton estate to live with both her illustrious lover and her husband in a *ménage à trois*. The waters of the Wandle fed a canal that was cut through the grounds, which Emma called 'The Nile' and which she stocked with waterfowl and fish. The house was sold following Nelson's death in the Battle of Trafalgar in 1805 and the estate gradually broke up; it is remembered now only in local street names.

The path emerges into a small car park, which you cross to go through an archway, at whose base are stones from the medieval Merton Priory. In Emma Hamilton's day, Merton was still a small village which had built up around the priory. Cross Merantun Way, which traverses the now defunct line of the 1869 rail route that linked Wimbledon and Tooting via Merton Park and gave a boost to local industries; continue down the path signed Morden Hall Park. Across the river on the left is a superb example of Arts and Crafts architecture – a house designed by architect J.R. Vyning in 1912. You have now reached Merton Abbey Mills, where you can capture something of the atmosphere of the past. Here, old mill buildings have been turned into craft markets and ethnic food stalls and the Liberty factory's Victorian waterwheel has been restored. In the museum you will discover more about the mills' history and about William Morris and the Arts and Crafts Movement.

From Merton Abbey Mills, return across Merantun Way along a riverside path to the front of the superstore and Merton High Street, then turn right to Colliers Wood Underground Station.

THE COUNTRY
WANDLE:
MORDEN–WADDON
PONDS

Summary: The route follows the Wandle through established parkland and snatches of countryside to one of its two present-day sources at Waddon Ponds. Explore the river's changing moods as it flows between concrete strait-jackets and rural meanders, bypasses industrial estates and the sites of former mills and factories. It flows through parkland, including Morden Hall and Beddington parks, which provides welcome relief from the surrounding suburbia.

Start:	Morden Road Tramline Station
Finish:	Waddon Railway Station
Distance:	7 miles (11.7km)
Refreshments:	Morden Hall Park; Surrey Arms, Morden Road; the Palmerston pub, Mill Lane

From Morden Road Tramline Station, take the exit that crosses beneath Morden Road, go up the steps and turn left. Just past the advertising billboards turn left down the sandy gravelled track signed Phipps Bridge; continue until the track opens onto the water meadows, then take a clear right turn signed Morden Hall Park.

Modern Hall Park
The path through the 125-acre (50-hectare) park first winds through Wandle wetlands, which are managed to create a valuable habitat for wetland birds, such as herons, plants and insects. Just after a wooden bridge there's a junction with a blue signpost: turn left here and look right over another small bridge towards an ornamental aqueduct, weir, lake and

Opposite: The wetlands, gardens and magnificent tree-lined avenues of Morden Hall Park are the first real taste of the rural delights that come after the suburbia and industry of the lower River Wandle.

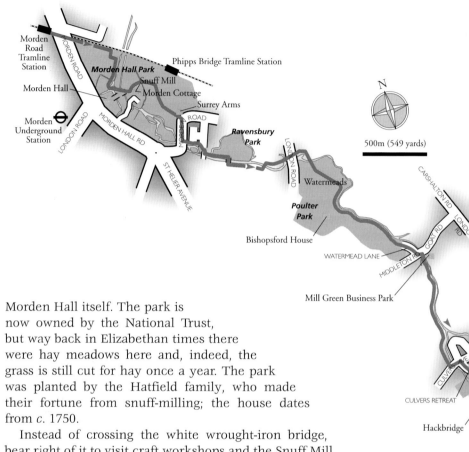

Morden Hall itself. The park is
now owned by the National Trust,
but way back in Elizabethan times there
were hay meadows here and, indeed, the
grass is still cut for hay once a year. The park
was planted by the Hatfield family, who made
their fortune from snuff-milling; the house dates
from *c*. 1750.

Instead of crossing the white wrought-iron bridge,
bear right of it to visit craft workshops and the Snuff Mill.
Snuff (ground tobacco) superseded chewing tobacco from
the early 18th century and was at its most popular during
the reign of George IV (1820–30). You can see the kilns
where the tobacco leaves were dried, a waterwheel on a
channel that diverts water from the Wandle and the great
millstones that ground the tobacco into a powder fine enough
to sniff. The last snuff was milled here in 1922.

Leaving the snuff factory, turn right to walk past white Morden Cottage
and a centuries-old yew tree and rejoin the main path through the park,
turning right along an avenue of stately limes and chestnuts. Follow the
avenue, which was planted in the 1870s, as it curves to the right, looking
left to admire a splendid weeping beech tree and, on reaching Morden
Road, turn right. There's a pub stop here at the Surrey Arms just to the left.

Ravensbury Park

Turn right and cross the road to rejoin the trail (signed Ravensbury Park) to the left just before the road crosses the river, then head immediately right through the gate in the railings. On the far bank is the site of Ravensbury Mill, partly replaced now by riverside housing, but the original buildings behind it are due to become the new Wandle Industrial Museum. Ravensbury was reputedly the river's last working mill. It produced snuff from 1755 to 1925 and during the Second World War was adapted to generate electricity and was occasionally used to power woodworking machinery. The Ravensbury Park of today is a remnant of one of Mitcham's four medieval manors. From the late 17th century to *c.* 1860, it was also a major player in the thriving local textile industry; towards the centre of the park there are traces of parallel watercourses, which were used for bleaching.

As you cross an iron-railed bridge to walk along the opposite bank of the river, straight ahead is a pair of millstones, now sadly defaced by graffiti,

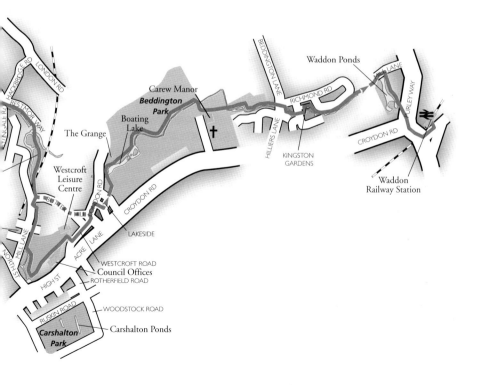

which were once turned by the horizontal cog wheel above. The path is lined by sturdy horse-chestnut trees, then on the left is one of the park's 200-year-old plane trees, with its impressive mottled trunk. The park is noted for its variety of trees. Keep right at this point and follow the broad, attractive stretch of river, which is popular with waterfowl. Look in the tree canopy for flocks of green parakeets that have naturalized in London, and on the river itself for the less welcome invader, floating pennywort, with its buttercup-like leaves; this pest of a plant overwhelms anything in its path. Bear right over an iron-railed bridge, passing some mature willows and the dark strata of a cedar tree, then veer round to the left, past three-storey flats, before reaching London Road.

The Meandering Wandle

Turn right, cross the road, pass over the river and head left down the path for Watermeads and Poulter Park. Through the railings on the opposite bank you can glimpse white weatherboarded millworkers' cottages of the 18th and 19th centuries. Follow the iron railings until you reach a fork, and take the right-hand option. This leads to a delightful rural curve in the river beneath Bishopsford House. All too soon, however, an industrial estate rears up on the east bank. In summer the path is invaded by Japanese knotweed (which resists most attempts at being curbed), hogweed, nettles, dock and the giant leaves and spiky-balled seed heads of giant burdock.

Hogweed

Negotiate an iron gate, taking note of the Wandle's energetic flow as it tumbles round the corner, and pass alongside the terraced cottages of Watermead Lane. Turn right and cross Goat Road. Cross the road and turn left off it just past a Neo-Georgian house. The Mill Green Business Park across the road was once a site for lavender and leather processing.

The next section is a bit grubby, with badly drained land to the right and occasional buildings on the left bank, although enlivened by cheerful paintings of dragonflies and other creatures on the walls of a factory. The broad, metalled path is flanked on the right by railings; where it forks, keep straight ahead and at the next junction turn right just before the footbridge to follow a short but slow and peaceful stretch of the river, where willowherb and yellow flag iris add summer colour. The closer you get to a rather run-down complex of flats, the less watercress there is in the river and the more rubbish. At the road, turn left then right down the residential cul-de-sac of Culvers Retreat, which is signposted Wandle Trail. The continuation of the path is obvious on the left just before the housing ends.

Wilderness Island

Cross a little humpback bridge, where the dreaded floating pennywort has taken hold, and turn immediately right, heading towards the green-arched road bridge. Turn right over the Hackbridge, cross Hackbridge Road and turn left to rejoin the Wandle. Pass a weir and continue along a metalled path with some fine plane trees, followed by scruffy woodland. On your left, at the confluence of the two branches of the Wandle, is a nature reserve managed by the London Wildlife Trust and aptly named Wilderness Island. The entrance is off Mill Lane, into which the path leads. Turn left along the lane, where it is signposted Carshalton Ponds.

Now you have the option of saving about 20 minutes of walking by turning left along Butter Hill. The principal route, however, is to continue straight ahead along the east bank of the river through a housing estate alleviated by silver birches. Turn right to cross the river at the bridge with concrete spheres (the Palmerston pub is just on the road ahead) and proceed along the west bank. Turn left at the next bridge to walk through the gardens towards Carshalton Ponds, one of the two main sources of the Wandle. The waters that feed the Wandle originate in the North Downs but filter through the chalk and travel underground until they bubble up in a series of springs between the South London border towns of Croydon and Carshalton. There was a time when the river flowed through what is now the centre of Croydon, but it is now confined to pipes and the two main branches of the river now emerge from Carshalton and Waddon Ponds.

Beddington Park

Take the park path to the left, past the red-brick council offices, and, after passing the children's playground and sports courts, turn left at the signpost for Beddington Park. Cross to the Westcroft Leisure Centre and turn right, then left along Westcroft Road. At the end, turn left and, after the pond with a fountain, cross the busy London Road (if you have taken the Butter Hill short cut, pick up the route from this point), then turn left into Lakeside, with its row of ponds. Keep straight ahead along a flagstoned path that leads to a car park. Go straight across this into Beddington Park, across the footbridge at the tip of Grange Lake. The park is recorded as the location of two manorial estates in the Domesday Book.

Turn right to follow the edge of the lake via a grotto. The formal gardens give way to open parkland, where you follow the track alongside the river. When you reach a main track that leads left to the sports grounds and tennis courts, turn left and then right to walk along the north bank of the river. At the next bridge, follow the signs to Waddon Ponds and at the end of a row of cottages go diagonally across the car park and a patch of green. Look back for a good view of Carew Manor, now an adult-education centre but for 500 years the home of the Carew family. Continue diagonally. At the fork just before a big cedar tree, turn right to follow the river, with a view ahead of a large block of flats. At the bridge, go right then left and head right towards the exit gate adorned with concrete spheres. Cross Beddington Lane, then turn left off it to follow the Wandle on your left and a brick wall on your right.

The path emerges into a small road, where there are some weatherboarded mill cottages that were attached to the nearby Lambert's snuff mill. Head for the fine Victorian factory building in front of you, turn left in front of it, then take first right into Kingston Gardens. Follow a strip of green between the river and a housing estate on the left. Watercress was grown commercially on the river here until the 1930s. The path turns back into a road again; continue along a patch of green with the river to your right. At the end, cross the river and turn left (signposted Waddon Ponds). Factory buildings lie to the left, tall willows to the right; then, on your right, are a playground and Waddon Ponds, source of the Croydon branch of the Wandle. The pond is the last remaining of several millponds that belonged to the manor of Waddon Court. Walk through the gardens, cross Purley Way and turn left to Waddon Railway Station.

RIBBON OF GREEN: THE BRENT RIVER

Summary: A surprising and delightful ribbon of green countryside winds through the roads, industrial estates and dense suburbia of north-west London. Though it has been notorious in the past for its pollution and still has problems today, the River Brent flows through a band of meadowland rather than the marsh and industrial landscape of the Lea in the east. We see evidence of the river's changing moods, from raging floodwaters to wildlife haven, and a splendid example of Victorian engineering in the Wharncliffe Viaduct at Hanwell.

Start:	Perivale Underground Station
Finish:	Hanwell Railway Station
Distance:	6 miles (10km)
Refreshments:	Hanwell village or take a picnic!

From Perivale Underground Station, turn left and continue to the footbridge that takes you over the A40 road and descends into a brief cul-de-sac. Cross Perivale Lane and almost immediately opposite is a lych gate to the footpath past the tiny weatherboarded church of St Mary the Virgin, which dates back to 1125. Soon after, cross the river and take the first path to the right. A brief detour right, down a gravel path, enables you to follow a single curve in the river at this point. Follow this path until it meets a junction and then turn right to cut a straight route to emerge on Argyle Road. Turn right along the road until you see a path leading onto the playing fields, where the river loops to the north. Cut obliquely across the fields to go behind the swimming pool, just beyond which you will meet the river once more at Ruislip Road East. Turn right under the railway bridge and immediately look for the escape route along a green path squeezed in between river and busy road. Perivale Park, on the opposite side of the river, used to be one of the biggest hay fields in Ealing when fodder was in great demand to feed the horses that drew London's barges, carriages and carts before the advent of steam power.

A Ribbon of Green
River and path swing south and you have to cross Ruislip Road East at Greenford Bridge and rejoin the riverside route obliquely opposite.

Suddenly, as the traffic noise recedes behind, a ribbon of green countryside emerges, which you can follow with only minor interruptions all the way to the River Thames at Brentford by linking with *A Flight of Locks* walk (see pages 20–26). Admittedly, if the river is low – and its level varies according to the season and the flow from Welsh Harp (or Brent) Reservoir upstream – its exposed banks will be littered with shreds of plastic and other rubbish. Occasionally, the locals form a working party to clear the river of its litter and now Ealing Council has hired a contractor to do the job full-time. Even at its worst, however, the condition of the river is a vast improvement on how it was at the turn of the century, when it was so polluted with raw effluent from sewage works at Wembley, Hendon and Hanwell that all the fish, and even the water rats, were killed off.

You can see how dramatically the river's flow changes by observing the deposits of shingle, the high, stepped terraces on the banks and the water-scoured vegetation. The Brent's waters are fed by streams coming from high gravel terraces to the north, such as Dollis Brook at Barnet, the Silk Stream in Edgware and the Wealdstone in Harrow. In 1901, serious flooding left the streets of Perivale under water. Stretches of the river were tamed and straightened to reduce downstream flooding. Today, the Brent's flow is controlled by sluice gates on the Welsh Harp Reservoir, which open and close automatically depending on the level of water. The reservoir was created in the 1830s by damming the Brent's upper waters and tributaries. Initially, its job was to provide water for the Grand Union and Regent's canals, flowing along a 4-mile (6.7-km) feeder channel that joins the Paddington Arm of the Grand Union (see pages 14–19, *Hay and Bricks* walk), but today it operates as a flood buffer. Even so, with particularly heavy rainfall the reservoir gets full to bursting point; at one point in 1977 the sluice gates were opened and 1,000 cubic feet (28 cubic metres) of water a second rushed into the already swollen Brent.

Riverside Meadows

So, after heavy rain and frequently in winter the riverside path is likely to be impassable. Then you must go up a bank reinforced with railway sleepers and turn right along a higher field. When the river is reduced to a low stream, however, you will be able to continue along the broad, flat, dry bank. Either way, you come to an expanse of meadow that is golden with wild grasses in summer, with splashes of purple from thickets of

Opposite: The Wharncliffe Viaduct at Hanwell was designed by Isambard Kingdom Brunel (1806–59) and erected around 1836 to take the railway over the Brent Valley. It is 300 yards (274m) long and 65 feet (19.8m) high.

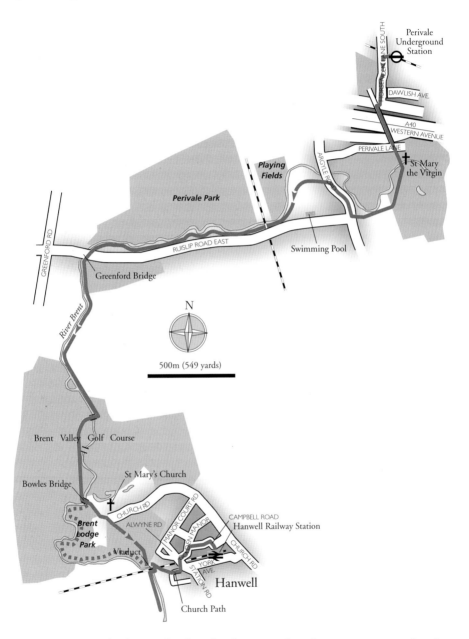

rosebay willowherb. Footbridges lead across the river – you can take the first or the second – to Brent Valley Golf Course, where you turn left to follow a sand and gravel track bordered by hawthorn until eventually arriving at the tubular metal Bowles Bridge, also known as Boles or Bulls Bridge. Stop awhile to read the information board on local wildlife, which highlights exciting summer visitors, such as spotted flycatchers and reed and sedge warblers, which feast on the waterside insects. Just after sunset on a summer's evening you may see pipistrelle bats flying in their high-speed, jerky manner, as a colony has chosen these water meadows as a foraging ground. A ditch nearby is evidence of the river's re-routing, for it marks a former course and is the only place in London where a particular species of willow grows that was once used in basket-making.

Brunel Makes His Mark

Across the bridge, turn right. Here you have a choice either to follow the river as it loops through meadows beneath Hanwell (turning right when you meet the metalled path) or taking a high-level route. For the high-level route bear left uphill towards St Mary's Church, which was designed by Sir George Gilbert Scott (1811–78) and completed in 1841; this stands on the site of the original settlement of Hanwell Village and an earlier 12th-century church. Cross the road obliquely in front of the church to enter Brent Lodge Park, which was converted from three big fields that were cultivated in rotation in medieval times. Walk along the avenue across the park.

The valley ahead is spanned by the imposing arches of a railway viaduct constructed in the 1830s by Isambard Kingdom Brunel (1806–59). At the far end of the park head right, downhill, along a narrow metalled path towards the viaduct. (If you took the alternative riverside route, this is where you end up.) Bear left to go through a wooden gate and beneath a towering arch to rejoin the river. To appreciate the full impact of the viaduct, cross the footbridge immediately ahead and walk along the broad grassy path above the river for a few yards before looking back at the great arches striding across the vale. It is said that when Queen Victoria was travelling by private train to Windsor, she asked for the train to stop on the viaduct so that she could enjoy the view of the Brent Valley. Her viewpoint would have been nearly 70 feet (22m) above the valley floor. The eight arches of the viaduct are supported by a pair of hollow brick piers and span 300 yards (274m), although the viaduct's supporting embankment stretches for a total of 1½ miles (2.5km) at the approaches. This is part of Brunel's 120-mile (200-km) Great Western Railway route from London to Bristol, and was his first major design to be completed.

Retrace your steps back across the footbridge and turn sharp right just before the viaduct up a narrow path into Church Path, left under another viaduct arch, right into Golden Manor and right again into Campbell Road, which leads to Hanwell Railway Station.

HARNESSING THE TIDE: THE BOW BACK RIVERS

Summary: In the amorphous muddle of industrial estates and housing between Stratford, Bromley and West Ham, is a network of tidal and semi-tidal rivers that feed into the River Lea. We explore the triangle of land that they enclose and find some gems of industrial history among the wasteland.

Start & Finish:	Bromley-by-Bow Underground Station
Distance:	3³⁄₄ miles (6.3km)
Refreshments:	Three Mills

From Bromley-by-Bow Underground Station, turn left to go alongside the main A12 Blackwall Tunnel Northern Approach Road. On the other side there's a supermarket, for which you are heading. Continue along the road until you see steps going down into the subway. Turn right out of the subway and the supermarket is opposite when you emerge at the top. Cross the road and follow the supermarket round to the right and into Three Mill Lane. You are now on Three Mills Island, an enclave of cobbled courtyards running between House Mill and Clock Mill on the right. They are all that survive of the many mills that once utilized the tidal power of the Bow Back Rivers.

Tidal waters and channels that once ebbed and flowed over salt-marsh were tamed and impounded through the ages to provide the network of channels that makes up the Bow Back Rivers. Their names – Pudding Mill River, City Mill River, Waterworks River – indicate their hard-working heritage. Once they were busy with barge traffic carrying coal, raw materials and goods to and from from the industries that developed along their banks in the 19th century. Now, waterway traffic is restricted to the occasional dredger, maintenance or refuse barge; what industries remain are no longer dependent upon the waterways they overlook.

Opposite: In the depths of Bromley and Stratford, there's an enclave of old millhouses on the tidal river at Three Mills. Here, among the evocative odours of mud and sea air, are the remnants of an ancient milling industry.

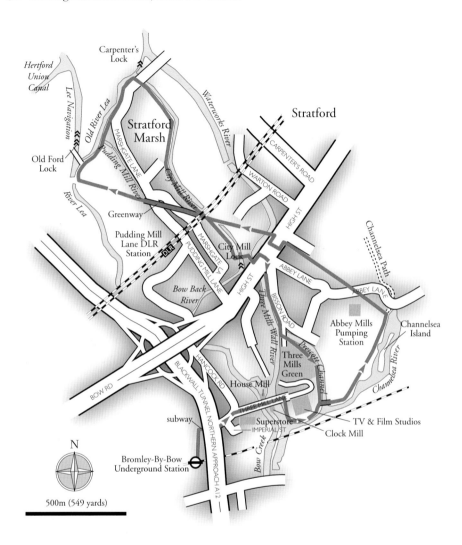

The rivers were first used for water transport in the 15th century, but, because they are tidal and heavily silted, they are now largely unnavigable and little used. The area can only improve – not least in view of London's bid to host the 2012 Olympic Games: in fact, work has already begun, as the area has been selected for restoration.

A Whiff of Gin

Take time to look back at the Three Mills buildings from the landscaped area to the right of the mill complex. From here you can look down into the mud-thick river, smell the salty air and see the millstream route beneath the buildings. At low tide there is little but a narrow ribbon of murky water worming its way through slopes of darkly gleaming mud. It was the power of the receding tide that was harnessed by these mills when they were in operation: as the tide came in (or 'was making'), water was channelled into the millrace and the floodgates beyond the mills were lowered to trap the incoming water; then, when the tide turned, the gates were raised and the outflow turned the waterwheels.

You can still see much of the internal mill machinery, including the huge waterwheels and six pairs of millstones, inside House Mill on the left of the cobbled courtyard. In its day, House Mill was one of the most powerful tidal mills in England; it last worked in 1941, but is now being restored as a listed industrial site. Long before the distillery business was established, corn was ground here and at many other sites locally – eight are recorded in the 1086 Domesday Book – helping the nearby village of Stratforde-atte-Bowe (modern Bow) to build up a reputation as the centre for providing London's bread. Three Mills was originally part of an abbey that was destroyed during Henry VIII's dissolution of the monasteries in the 1530s. The two surviving mills became privately owned and one was turned over to grinding gunpowder in 1588. In the 18th century came the establishment of a distillery business combined with a piggery, which supplied the British Navy with pork.

The tide-powered millstones ground grain for gin over a period of 165 years from the 18th century. The alcoholic connection continued into the 20th century: Clock Mill, with its on-site oast house for drying grain, was, until recent decades, the headquarters of the wine and spirit arm of Bass Brewers; the present building dates from 1817.

Desolate Charm

Keeping House Mill to your left, continue to the film studios at the bottom of the cobbled path. Turn right to pass along the side of Clock Mill and follow the path round to the left along the course of the Channelsea River. The bright mural with its overlay of rather stylish graffiti adds welcome colour to what can be a bleak spot on a cold, grey day, while in early summer blue periwinkle may be in bloom on the bank to your left a little further on. Gasometer shells dating from 1870, built on the site of an 18th-century factory that made military rockets for the Napoleonic wars, rise on the far bank to the right and the river is impounded with concrete girders. Wind blows in from the sea, mingling with intense odours of tidal mud and traffic fumes. Nevertheless, on a blue day, even this prospect has its desolate charms.

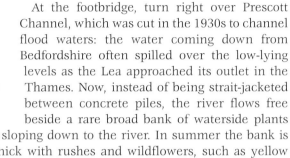

Yellow flag iris

At the footbridge, turn right over Prescott Channel, which was cut in the 1930s to channel flood waters: the water coming down from Bedfordshire often spilled over the low-lying levels as the Lea approached its outlet in the Thames. Now, instead of being strait-jacketed between concrete piles, the river flows free beside a rare broad bank of waterside plants sloping down to the river. In summer the bank is thick with rushes and wildflowers, such as yellow flag iris, purple willowherb and Himalayan balsam, and the footpath is bordered by native shrubby trees, such as dogwood, hazel, guelder rose and rowan. Channelsea Island, which lies midstream, is seriously polluted, although primary woodland birch trees grow there. Through them you may see the skeletal remains of the chemical factory that was responsible for poisoning the ground. It is gratifying that, since those heavily polluted days (another part of the factory on the far bank produced sulphuric acid), fish such as pike, perch and eel have returned to these waters.

The Cathedral of Sewage

Along this stretch you catch your first glimpse of a grey, slate-roofed building with a Neo-Gothic Victorian red and green central tower. This is the 'Cathedral of Sewage' or, more strictly, Abbey Mills Pumping Station, which we'll soon pass. Meanwhile, pass pumping-station relics: a hump of massive pipe and, at the top of the rise, the sculptural iron 'snail', part of the works machinery. Turn right past the 'snail' and left along a metalled path that leads above the pumping station, the former operating centre of an innovatory Victorian sewage system. You are now walking along the Greenway, the flattering name for the course of the Northern Outfall Sewer, a mighty pipe that 'intercepted' waste from throughout north and west London and carried it to be discharged into the Thames east of the City. At first, the waste was untreated as it flowed into the Thames; the pipes still carry sewage to this day, but happily it is now treated at a plant in Beckton to the south-east.

The network of interceptor sewage pipes was devised by metropolitan engineer Sir Joseph Bazalgette (1819–91) and was the first effective step towards solving London's dreadful problems of flooding cesspits, foul-smelling rivers running with raw sewage and frequent outbreaks of cholera. Bazalgette, who was also responsible for the Victoria and Albert and Chelsea Embankments (see pages 149–158, *Bridging the Thames* walk), was almost a local, as, despite his unusual name, he was born upstream at Enfield.

Continue along the Greenway to Stratford High Street. The locality earned the name of 'Stinky Stratford' when it became the focus of industries escaping the anti-pollution laws of metropolitan London in the mid-19th century. Here, instead of the Thames, it was the Bow Back Rivers that took the uncontrolled, untreated flow of industrial effluent.

We want to continue along the Greenway on the opposite side of the road, but to do this you need to turn left to cross the road at the traffic lights and back on yourself to go left under the iron arch. On the left is a 1930s building with a tiled mural of flower sellers. After a short stretch on the Greenway above industrial wasteland, there's an unpleasant but brief diversion down steps to a path, turning right through a tunnel under the railway line and back up a narrow path to the Greenway. Equilibrium is soon restored, at least in summer, by healthy bushes of creamy dog rose. Continue until the Greenway crosses the Lee Navigation at its meeting with the Old River Lea and look down to old warehouses and Old Ford Lock (not to be confused with the other Old Ford Lock on the Regent's Canal).

Locks and Bridges

Retrace your path and go right down some steps and right again beneath a pair of seriously big, black sewer pipes and a bridge carrying a commemorative plaque to Bazalgette's Northern Outfall Sewer. Continue along the towpath towards Old Ford Lock, which is immediately ahead. At the lock, keep right of the footbridge and go beneath another couple of sewer pipes, along a pleasantly rural stretch that follows the old river. Look out for kingfishers! A humped footbridge, ridged to give barge horses grip, arches over Pudding Mill River, which enters from the right. The poor old Pudding Mill is now clogged up with floating pennywort: this invasive plant blots out the vital light and oxygen that other plant and animal life needs to survive; the only sure way to get rid of it is to rip it out and burn it.

Soon after, Carpenter's Lock lies ahead, sadly neglected although restoration is promised. Immediately after another humped bridge, turn right and cross over Marshgate Lane. We are now following the City Mill River as it sweeps in a curve to the right, with a view of Canary Wharf in the distance. Nature is reasserting itself here with banks of watercress and reed beds. We skirt the winding hole – a clogged-up basin that was once a turning point for barges – pass under a railway bridge and beneath a section of the Greenway that you walked along earlier. Shortly after reaching a new waterside residential development, cross the Bow Back River, which leads off to the right, and the Waterworks River, which until the mid-20th century would have been a busy crossroads for cargo-carrying barges.

Where the road meets Stratford High Street once more, turn left to cross to Abbey Lane, then immediately right to follow the towpath along Three Mills Wall River (signposted House Mill). It's hard to imagine now, but in the early 19th century, this stretch must have been quite pleasant, lined as it was with osier beds, which produced the raw materials for basket-making. Unfortunately, factories producing printing inks, glue and asphalt that had been banned from operating in London under an 1844 Pollution Act soon moved out to the Lea Valley.

Enter the pleasant Three Mills Green and head straight for a dramatic sculpture of clasped hands immediately before you. Alternatively, you can bear right to follow the river straight back to Three Mills, but the sculpture is rather moving, as it commemorates people who died in the course of their work on the waterways, including a Customs and Excise officer and another 1901 victim who was 'overcome by foul air... and those who descended to save him suffered the same death'.

Walk along the east side of the green space bordered with horse-chestnut trees and, from late spring, generous clumps of bugloss and comfrey. You can see Abbey Mills Pumping Station to your left. Circuit or go up and over the sudden mound, go past the allotments on the far side of the Prescott Channel, turning right at the footbridge to retrace your steps from the start of the walk back to Bromley-by-Bow Underground Station.

THE LEA'S MARSHY ORIGINS: LEA RIVER LOOP AND HACKNEY

Summary: Discover the Old River Lea and how humans have tamed it in the service of transport and industry and in order to control the floods that have plagued the river's lower levels. As a London waterway system, the Lea is second in importance only to the Thames and has provided a key transport and communications route, a focus for waterside industries, a source of rich meadows for cultivation and grazing and a vital water supply for the city and its suburbs. It is also an important leisure facility for Londoners. Make sure you do this walk at a weekend to take advantage of the Middlesex Filter Beds Nature Reserve, an evocative blend of industrial ruins reclaimed by wildlife.

Start and Finish:	Hackney Wick Railway Station
Distance:	6 miles (10km)
Refreshments:	Pubs at Lea Bridge; café at Springfield Marina

From the station, turn left and then left again at Carpenter's Road. Just over the bridge, cross the road and turn right to go down to the towpath, then right to go back under the road.

A Rural Feel

The waterway here is broad and still. Look closely into the shallow waters and you can see waterweed and shadowy brown fish. Look out for cycling fishermen, dragging their lines behind them as they pedal the towpath. There's the occasional island of water lilies, too (if they're not in flower, you can identify the white species, *Nymphaea alba*, because its leaves float, while the yellow species, *Nuphar lutea*, has some submerged leaves). There's little of note to see for a half a mile (835m) or so, although we're walking along the relatively green side, which in early summer is laced in parts with elderflower and cow parsley; on the opposite bank is housing, together with light industrial and office buildings. After passing the red-brick pile of a Victorian school building on the far bank and a road bridge, our path broadens out into a strip of green; apart from the ebbing and flowing burr of traffic, you could almost be in the countryside.

The next major road crossing is Homerton Road (you will return to this point at the end of the walk to retrace your steps to Hackney Wick Railway Station). Now the route is even greener, with playing fields on the right, though less bucolic stretches are dominated by the invasive Japanese knotweed. In high summer, the sluggish waters may be in danger of deoxygenating, as they are covered with duckweed, broken only by splashes of colour provided, unfortunately, by floating carrier bags and cans. This is the Hackney Cut stretch of the Lee Navigation – the name for the channelled rather than the natural course of the old River Lea – and we are passing along the edge of Hackney Marsh. To add the word 'marsh' is tautological, for the word Hackney comes from *haca's eoth,* meaning 'well-watered land or marsh'. The marsh became a public open space in 1894. For centuries it had been 'lammas land', that is, it could be cultivated by those who had a share in it only between 6 April and 12 August, while for the rest of the year it was common land for grazing. Today, much of the marshland has been largely filled in and transformed into playing fields fringed by trees.

A Bid For Clean Water

We pass under another road bridge, where local road names, such as Millfields, recall the many mills of the 18th century, many of which were destroyed by fire in 1791. Over to the left, a big red-brick warehouse, which later became a refuse disposal depot, is followed by a bridge enclosed in grey corrugated iron. A curving wall echoes the course of the towpath. Beyond it are the Middlesex Filter Beds, now a nature reserve and a magical retreat where the old channels, beds and paths of a defunct water-treatment works are half buried beneath natural vegetation. The filter beds were built in a bid to purify the River Lea's water supply following the 1849 cholera epidemic that claimed the lives of 14,000 East Londoners. The evocative industrial memorabilia includes rails, a sand trolley, sluice gates, the central filtering culvert and dried-up channels and tanks. Water treatment ceased in 1969 and now this haven attracts more than 60 species of birds, including some that stop here for a rest on their migration routes, while crevices in the brick and concrete provide cosy hibernation spots for amphibians.

From the main entrance, which is on the right just before the bridge over the Navigation, follow the nature reserve path to the left and then go

Opposite: At the Middlesex Filter Beds Nature Reserve, the River Lea's waters are still governed by sluices, although it looks like a real river. Two hundred years ago this area was awash with mills.

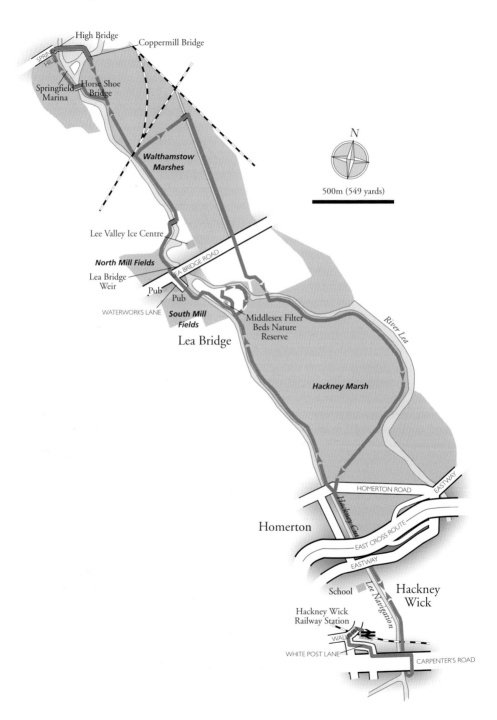

right, to where the Old River Lea is flowing free of the Navigation. The river's waters are still governed by sluices, but here it begins to look like a real river. You can see nothing of them now, but back in the 18th century there were busy mills on this site. The brisk, channelled flow fed waterwheels to power the boring of tree trunks to make the precursors of iron water pipes. A second mill ground grain and the energy from a third powered machinery to sharpen pins and needles (the needles were then shipped to Worcestershire to have eyes inserted). The locks and sluices that controlled the water level and flow were good news for the milling business, but put the millers at odds with the boatmen who wanted clear, direct waterways to and from London; the Hackney Cut was dug between here and Old Ford to bypass the mills and bring a halt to the arguing.

Divergence and Convergence

After circuiting the nature reserve, return to the gate you entered by and turn right back onto the towpath. Cross the steep footbridge, with its treads or 'scorchers' for horses, onto the left bank and turn right along the towpath over another footbridge. Look across the water to the right to a weir blocked by tilting barges laden with rubbish: beneath unusual overhead 'guillotine'-style lock gates, the Old River Lea breaks away from the Navigation.

There are pub stops here on the waterside and up on the road. Continue along the towpath past a recreation ground and follow the united waters of the river and the Navigation in a broad sweep to the right, passing warehouses and gibbet-like gantries projecting over the river. Shortly you cross the river over another ridged footbridge and take a high gravel path bordering Walthamstow Marshes. Continue under the railway bridge until you reach the next bridge (Horse Shoe Bridge), pass a café and cross the water again over Coppermill Bridge to skirt Springfield Marina and cross High Bridge. Follow the track leading left out of the marina. It is possible then to take a right turn, improbably signposted to Lee Valley Ice Centre (which is near Lea Bridge), and wend your way, via a network of paths, in a generally eastward direction. You need to cut back to the waterside path just before the railway bridge you came under before. The simpler, but perhaps less interesting, route is to take an even sharper right from the marina exit and return to Horse Shoe Bridge, then retrace your steps left along the path back to the railway bridge.

The marshes are rich in waterside plants, including yellow flag iris and creamy meadowsweet, followed by purple loosestrife and Michaelmas daisies in late summer. When the water table is high, you can get an impression of the waterlogged channels, their courses marked by reeds and sedges, which are traces of meltwater courses formed at the end of the last Ice Age.

Over Marsh and Meadow

Go under the railway bridge and turn immediately left along a boardwalk over the marshes. At the end of the boardwalk, continue straight ahead over grazing meadows, where you may see old English Longhorns and Belted Galloway cattle. The animals have been reintroduced after a 100-year absence and hay is cut to maintain the distinctive ecosystem that has evolved here from a combination of wild and managed land. The first major impact on the water level came in AD 896, when King Alfred the Great ordered both damming and draining of the Lea Levels at various points to alter the course of the upstream river and make it too shallow to be navigated by the Danish invaders. This enterprise, plus the cutting of additional drainage channels over the centuries, turned the marsh into meadowland. From the Middle Ages, this area was lammas land, until common grazing ceased around a century ago.

Across the meadow, climb to a metalled path that follows the course of an aqueduct, until you find a right turn over a footbridge that crosses the Old River Lea just below the Middlesex Filter Beds Nature Reserve; at the bridge you can look back to the weir. At the playing fields, turn left to join a path alongside the Old River Lea. Look out for an option to turn off the metalled road and follow a woody trail beneath trees, hugging the broad, clear, winding course of the old river. The riverside path rejoins the metalled road eventually and the sound of traffic begins to intrude upon the peace. Soon after, there's an entrance to a car park on the right. Take it and cross the recreation ground diagonally to the far left-hand corner. This brings you to Homerton Road, which you cross to rejoin the Lee Navigation. To return to Hackney Wick Railway Station, leave the Navigation after you've passed under a cluster of road and rail bridges and see the sign for the Hertford Union Canal and Old Ford Locks. Return to the road and turn left along Carpenter's Road, then right to return to the station.

Purple loosestrife

RURAL BROOKS: DOLLIS, FOLLY AND MUTTON

Summary: This is a nature ramble of a walk, offering rich tree-spotting opportunities. As the vale roller-coasters gently through unseen surrounding suburbs, you get an idea of how the landscape of the London basin was formed millions of years ago. If the weather forecast is good, take a picnic, for there are plenty of spots to stop at and no riverside cafés. Although the route threads its way through suburbs, such as Totteridge and Hampstead Garden Suburb, with their own interesting stories, these are hidden beyond the green vale of the walk. It is an all-weather route, as the path is mostly metalled. There are various points at which you can stop and start the walk.

Start:	High Barnet Underground Station
Finish:	East Finchley Underground Station
	(or various undergrounds en route)
Distance:	6 or 9 miles (10 or 15km)
Refreshments:	Old Red Lion, Barnet; many shops just off the route

In the Wake of the Sea

The Dollis and Mutton brooks rise on remnants of the clay and gravel ridges that are a feature of the London Basin landscape. Fifty million years ago, a warm tropical sea covered all of southern England and, as it retreated, the clays that had settled on its floor were left behind. There was a great river, too, in the broad, shallow vale, and over the next million years its sluggish waters, heavy with sand and mud carried from upstream waters, flooded the plain. Gradually the climate changed, the land rose and the river shrank, leaving layers of sand and gravel in its wake. Over further aeons of geological time, later watercourses scoured the layers of clay and sand, remnants of which can be seen in the high spots of what are now London suburbs, such as Highgate (where Mutton Brook rises), Totteridge (to the north of which lies the Dollis watershed), Hampstead Heath and, south of the present course of the Thames, Shooter's Hill, near Blackheath.

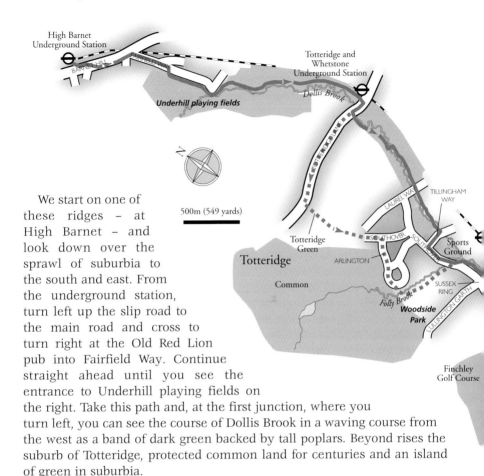

We start on one of these ridges – at High Barnet – and look down over the sprawl of suburbia to the south and east. From the underground station, turn left up the slip road to the main road and cross to turn right at the Old Red Lion pub into Fairfield Way. Continue straight ahead until you see the entrance to Underhill playing fields on the right. Take this path and, at the first junction, where you turn left, you can see the course of Dollis Brook in a waving course from the west as a band of dark green backed by tall poplars. Beyond rises the suburb of Totteridge, protected common land for centuries and an island of green in suburbia.

Visions of an Ancient Forest

When you reach the brook take the left fork, as the Dollis abruptly changes its course to flow southwards. Look back towards High Barnet and imagine the land covered in the oak woodland of the pre-glacial Great Middlesex Forest. The name Barnet means a clearing burnt in the woods, harking back to the Saxons' slash-and-burn techniques as they destroyed vast tracts of Britain's ancient forests. As the metalled path wends its way through stretches of well-maintained grass, or threads through wooded glades, the mood is more or less set for the entire walk. The dark shades of oak, elder, alder and dogwood are set off by the silvered greys and greens of willow and poplar. The Dollis, however, is out of sight for much of the way, enshrouded by a thick cover of nettles and shrubs, though you catch a glimpse of the occasional meander. In summer the flow is too slow and shallow to provide clear waters.

Your route straight ahead is clear to the first road crossing of Totteridge Lane. A possible stop/start point at Totteridge and Whetstone Underground Station is a short way to the left. Turn right and cross the road opposite the handful of shops to follow the opposite side of the brook. The heart of Totteridge – an extraordinary enclave of common land and charming detached houses, more like a Buckinghamshire village than a London suburb – is way up the hill to your right. It is possible to make a lengthy detour (marked on the map with broken lines) via the common, a 'village' pond and Folly Brook, a trickle of a Dollis tributary; but this will add a good 40 minutes to your journey and is likely to be very muddy in winter. To do the detour, walk up the road

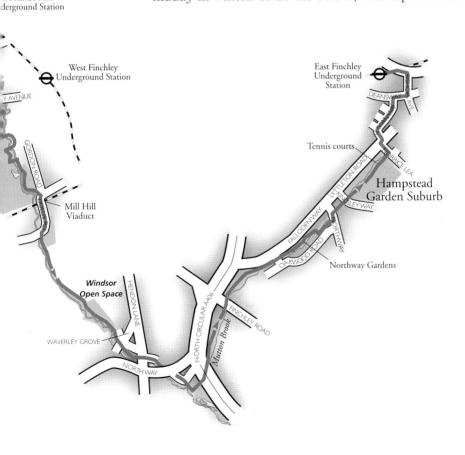

Woodside Park
derground Station

West Finchley
Underground Station

Y AVENUE

GORDON ROAD

Mill Hill
Viaduct

Windsor
Open Space

HENDON LANE

WAVERLEY GROVE

NORTHWAY

NORTH CIRCULAR A406

Mutton Brook

FINCHLEY ROAD

East Finchley
Underground
Station

DEANSWA AVE

Tennis courts

LYTTLETON ROAD

RRICE LEA

Hampstead
Garden Suburb

FALLODEN WAY

NORTHWAY

SLEY WAY

OAKWOOD ROAD

Northway Gardens

Dogwood

right until Totteridge Green and turn left. Continue to the pond, and take the path under the wooden arch into Southover, then head right down Arlington and right again. Turn right down a track between houses just after the bend at the bottom of the hill and follow the track left, then right across Folly Brook. Turn left and follow the valley back to the high wire fence at Southover. Cross the road and pick up the main walk at Woodside Park.

Dollis Meets Folly

The direct route after crossing Totteridge Lane meanders with the Dollis along a delightful broad and gently rolling valley. A white-barred gate announces the next road crossing – Laurel Way – into Riverside Walk and a pleasant park and playground area. At the end of this, turn right into Tillingham Way and continue to the junction with the broad Southover. (Alternatively, there's another stop/start point left along Tillingham Way, then right and left to Woodside Park Underground Station.) Pass the football ground on your left and, at a high wire fence, turn left into Woodside Park, the point at which the Folly and Dollis meet.

Cross the roads of Lullington Garth. Here, the valley closes in a bit, but the path continues along a band of green. After crossing Fursby Avenue (where you can turn left towards West Finchley Underground Station), the trees close in on the path as it follows the course of the Dollis, now set between steep banks carved by floodwaters. To the right are glimpses of Finchley Golf Course. Follow the stream and at the footbridge turn left to cross it. There's a pond on the right, which you must keep to your right. Where the path forks, go right and cross another bridge (a left fork here would take you to Gordon Road). Cross the next bridge – the pond is still on your right – and turn immediately left. Wind through the trees until you meet Dollis Road. Turn right and immediately before you is Mill Hill Viaduct.

Opposite: Compared to the mighty docks, the River Thames and the hard-working suburban rivers, the Mutton Brook is tiny and purely decorative as it flows through the parkland bordering Hampstead Garden Suburb.

A Victorian Marvel

Sadly, our only view of the viaduct is from the road, but look up left and right for a wonderful perspective of its 13 elegant arches. The viaduct was built in 1867 to carry a section of the London North Eastern Railway, which terminated at Liverpool Street, but now carries the underground's Northern Line. Cross the road before the blind bend and, just after crossing the Dollis, turn left to rejoin the riverside path. Continue through to a broad basin of more parkland, which is known as Windsor Open Space. Across Waverley Grove there are healthy clumps of comfrey. The path dips beneath Hendon Lane, through a slightly soiled but very short underpass, and suddenly the Dollis is almost river-like as it passes over a big concrete-stepped weir. Proceed under North Way and at the far end of a triangle of green turn left. This clear junction of streams, where the Mutton joins the Dollis from the east, is where Dollis Brook is no more: it becomes the Brent River and heads south, then west, to the Welsh Harp (Brent) Reservoir.

We, however, are following Mutton Brook to the east, and a pretty stretch it is too, like a microcosm of rural southern England – apart from the roar of traffic from the arterial roads that border it and which we keep encountering; Finchley Road is the first. At the end of an all-too-brief patch of tree-lined meadow, turn left over a footbridge and right up to Falloden Way. Walk along this busy road, past a tiny patch of wildlife and gardens on the right, past the entrance to Oakwood Road, across the road bridge over the brook, then turn right to rejoin the stream on its left bank.

Through Park and Garden

From now on, the route is through more formal municipal parks. Simply follow the course of the brook through Northway Gardens, across Northway and then Kingsley Way. You can take any of the eastward routes through the park; if you follow the stream you pass apartment blocks, the style of which reflects the spirit of Hampstead Garden Suburb, which borders the park to the south. The suburb was created from 1907 onwards, when the underground reached Golder's Green, and was the inspiration of Dame Henrietta Barnett, who envisaged a perfectly balanced community with a range of traditional English building styles and sizes, from craftsmen's cottages to Georgian-style mansions.

When you see the tennis courts at the far end of the park, head towards the exit into Norrice Lea; cross over Lyttleton Road, turn right then first left and follow Vivian Way all the way round to its junction with Deansway. Turn right and then left along Bishops Avenue and finally left at the junction to East Finchley Underground Station.

BRIDGING THE THAMES: WESTMINSTER– SOUTHWARK RETURN

Summary: There was a time when one of the most efficient ways of crossing the Thames at anywhere but London Bridge was to 'take the water' and hail a passing wherry or, if you had goods to transport, a lighter. We go on foot to find out more about watermen and lightermen and pass many of the bridges that they feared would make them redundant. We skim the culture-packed South Bank, pausing only to delve more deeply into buildings that have been influenced by or have some connection with the river.

Start and Finish:	Westminster Underground Station
Distance:	4 miles (6.7km)
Refreshments:	Royal Festival Hall; Gabriels Wharf; Victoria Embankment Gardens.

Monuments of Church and State

From the Bridge Street exit of Westminster Underground Station, in the shadow of the Clock Tower – better known as Big Ben, for its 16-ton bell – turn right and cross the road at the statue of Winston Churchill into Parliament Square. Walk the length of the Houses of Parliament on your left. Across the road you can see St Margaret's Westminster, the late medieval church of the House of Commons and the burial place of Elizabethan adventurer and explorer Sir Walter Raleigh (*c*. 1552–1618).

The Houses of Parliament are built on the site of William the Conqueror's Palace of Westminster, but most of the current buildings are the 19th-century Gothic revival confection of architects Charles Barry (1795–1860) and Augustus Pugin (1812–52), who went to town on the decorative features. Access to the river frontage here, at Lambeth Reach, is confined to politicians and friends, who sip summer sundowners on the terraces beneath striped awnings – red for Lords, green for Commons. In 1605 the Reach was the point at which Guy Fawkes (1570–1606) and his fellow Catholic conspirators in the Gunpowder Plot crossed the river with the aim of blowing up king and Parliament during that year's State opening.

After you pass the 'Sovereign's Entrance' of Victoria Tower, turn left to walk through Victoria Tower Gardens, where there is a statue of the suffragette Emmeline Pankhurst (1858–1928). Further on you pass a Gothic-style fountain memorial to Thomas Buxton, a leading figure in the abolition of the trade in African slaves – a move that affected many of the West India merchants dealing with plantation owners. Go up the steps at the end of the gardens and turn left over Lambeth Bridge. Until the 19th century, the only river crossing here was by horse ferry, hence Horseferry Road, the north-bank approach. The present 1932 structure replaced an earlier rusting and unsafe suspension bridge and is painted red, the livery of the House of Lords, while Westminster Bridge downstream is Commons green. At the pineapple-topped obelisks that mark each end of Lambeth Bridge, turn left onto the Albert Embankment, which, together with Victoria and Chelsea Embankments on the north side of the river, was masterminded by Sir Joseph Bazalgette, Chief Engineer to the Metropolitan Board of Works. Not only did Sir Joseph dramatically transform the appearance of the riverside, confining the Thames to a narrower, safer and more orderly course, but he also incorporated road, underground and sewage services.

Immediately on your right, across the road, is the red-brick Lambeth Palace, the London seat of the Archbishop of Canterbury. In times past, at high tide, the river reached its entrance. Adjacent to the Archbishop's Palace is the Tradescant Museum of Garden History, formerly St Mary's Church. The museum is named after the 17th-century explorer-botanists John Tradescant the elder (d. 1637) and his son, who was also called John (1608–62), both of whom are buried in the grounds. The elder Tradescant travelled to Europe and Russia and introduced many new plants to Britain, including summer-flowering jasmine and the Persian lilac. His son made several trips to America, bringing back such plants as *Aquilegia Canadensis, Rudbeckia laciniata* and many trees and shrubs. The tomb of Admiral William Bligh (1754–1817), former captain of HMS *Bounty*, is also here.

Doing the Lambeth Walk

Some say that the name Lambeth suggests that this was a landing place for sheep, others that the 'beth' relates, rather appropriately, to the Archbishop, as it comes from the Hebrew word meaning 'a sacred place'. In the 17th and 18th centuries, what is now the flagstoned Lambeth Walk was a stretch of shore broken by wooden wharves and overlooked by tumbledown houses, timber and boat yards, with mills and potteries behind. Continue to Westminster Bridge, which you come to next. To see the great lion that guards the bridge you must go up the steps and cross the road. The lion was sculpted from coadestone made at a local factory in 1837 to Ms Eleanor Coade's secret recipe, which has since been lost. If you don't want to see the lion, keep straight along the path under the bridge.

Jasmine

The Westminster Bridge of 1750 became London's second bridging point after London Bridge. Until this time, there was only a wooden bridge at Putney until Kingston. The construction of the original Westminster Bridge was opposed by City bankers and merchants, who were afraid it would take business away from their part of town. The bridge was also sabotaged by watermen who operated the cross-river ferries and plagued by financial problems, bad weather and even a small earthquake. Not surprisingly, perhaps, the bridge took 10 years to build. Over the next 100 years, though, its foundations were weakened by river currents and the original bridge was replaced by the present-day cast-iron one in 1862.

There is no need for route instructions now; you just continue along the Queen's Walk (marking Elizabeth II's Silver Jubilee in 1977), passing the grey mass of the former County Hall buildings, which were designed by Ralph Knott between 1908 and 1922, and are now home to fast-food restaurants, the Saatchi Gallery, the London Aquarium and booking offices for the London Eye. Then comes the giant ferris wheel itself. Jubilee Gardens lies beyond, with the 1963 Shell Centre behind. The striking Hungerford footbridges, which run on either side of the iron rail bridge, were completed in 2001. They are the second suspension footbridges to be constructed at this point. The first footbridge, whose piers still support the railway bridge, was designed by Isambard Kingdom Brunel, whose father Marc produced the rather less savoury pedestrian crossing of the Thames Tunnel (see pages 100–110, *Wharves and Warehouses* walk).

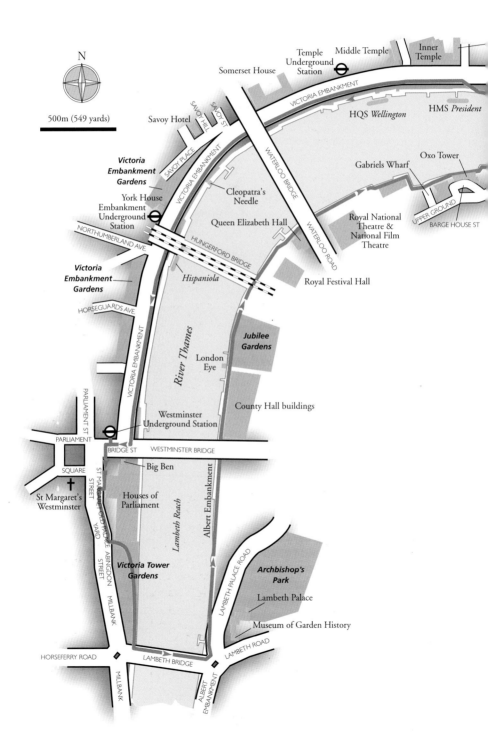

N

500m (549 yards)

Temple
Underground   Middle Temple   Inner
Station   Temple
Somerset House

VICTORIA EMBANKMENT

HQS *Wellington*   HMS *President*

Savoy Hotel

Oxo Tower

Gabriels Wharf

Victoria
Embankment
Gardens

Cleopatra's
Needle

UPPER GROUND

York House
Embankment
Underground
Station

Queen Elizabeth Hall

Royal National
Theatre &
National Film
Theatre

BARGE HOUSE ST

NORTHUMBERLAND AVE

HUNGERFORD BRIDGE

WATERLOO ROAD

Victoria
Embankment
Gardens

Hispaniola

Royal Festival Hall

HORSEGUARDS AVE

River Thames

Jubilee
Gardens

London
Eye

County Hall buildings

VICTORIA EMBANKMENT

PARLIAMENT ST

Westminster
Underground Station

PARLIAMENT

BRIDGE ST   WESTMINSTER BRIDGE

SQUARE

Big Ben

St Margaret's
Westminster

Houses of
Parliament

Lambeth Reach

Albert Embankment

ST MARGARET
OLD PALACE

ABINGDON STREET

*Victoria Tower
Gardens*

*Archbishop's
Park*

Lambeth Palace

LAMBETH PALACE ROAD

MILLBANK

Museum of Garden History

HORSEFERRY ROAD   LAMBETH BRIDGE

LAMBETH ROAD

MILLBANK

ALBERT EMBANKMENT

SAVOY HILL
SAVOY PLACE
SAVOY ST

VICTORIA EMBANKMENT

WATERLOO BRIDGE

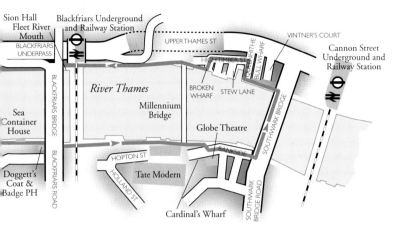

The City's Cultural Hub

Enjoy downstream views of the river as you follow the curve beneath Waterloo Bridge, passing the 1951 Royal Festival Hall, which was built for the Festival of Britain, Queen Elizabeth Hall, the National Film Theatre and, after the bridge, the National Theatre, which was built amid much controversy in the 1970s. The first Waterloo Bridge, which opened in 1816, was originally called Strand Bridge, but was renamed on the second anniversary of the Duke of Wellington's famous victory over the French. Once again, the scouring force of the river's tides and currents undermined the foundations and the bridge was closed in the 1920s. A new bridge was begun in 1937, but the outbreak of the Second World War delayed work, and the concrete piers were bomb-damaged. Nevertheless, the bridge opened in 1945 and, with its 1,250-foot (380-m) span, it is the longest of London's bridges.

Gabriels Wharf, with its *trompe-l'oeil* paintings, cafés and craft shops, is an attractive refreshment stop. Continue, passing the Art Deco Oxo Tower on your right (you can take a lift to a viewing gallery on the top floor), passing the river frontage of Sea Container House to Blackfriars Bridge.

Just before the bridge is the Doggett's Coat and Badge pub, interesting more for its name than its appearance. Thomas Doggett was an Irish actor and comedian who was so inspired by the Thames watermen and their practice of racing each other from one pick-up point to another, that in 1715 he founded an annual sculling race that is still held to this day. The course, running from London Bridge to Chelsea, is over 4 miles (6.7km) long, and is 'a test of watermenship and endurance, which... are the qualities required of a man who is going to get his living... as a waterman or lighterman'. The winner is awarded, as in times past, with a silver arm badge, scarlet coat and breeches – a 'Livery and Buttons and Appurtenances to it' – based on the uniform of an 18th-century waterman. The Company of Watermen and Lightermen was established in 1555 to introduce some control over the service that was so essential to the movement of goods and people.

Continue beneath Blackfriars Bridge, with its archive lithographs of bridge designs reproduced on the tiles. Look back to see the piers of polished granite and fancy capitals of Joseph Cubitt's design. The bridge was built in the 1860s and was widened *c.* 1910. Still standing in the river are chunky piers: all that remain of the original rail bridge. The end columns, topped by the cast-iron insignia of the London Chatham and Dover Railway Company, which was responsible for the original 1864 rail crossing, are fine examples of the ornate painted ironwork so beloved of the Victorians.

The Rebirth of Bankside

You are now walking along the stretch called Bankside, the focus of South Bank entertainment in the 16th and 17th centuries, when bear-baiting, cavorting with 'working girls' in the stews (saunas) and, of course, drama (at the Globe Theatre) were the main attractions. Now there is the Tate Modern, an art gallery housed in the former Bankside Power Station, which was designed by Sir Giles Gilbert Scott (1880–1960), completed in 1952 and closed 30 years later. The suspended walkway of the Millennium Bridge laid claim to being the first footbridge across the London Thames for 100 years, but it had to close soon after its opening because it was unstable; happily, it is now reinforced and in use. Shortly after the footbridge, look right to a row of 17th-century houses at Cardinal's Wharf, purportedly named after Cardinal Wolsey (*c.* 1474–1530), Lord Chancellor to King Henry VIII. It was in one of these houses that the architect Christopher Wren lived during the building of St Paul's Cathedral. Next is the Globe Theatre, lovingly reconstructed to be as close as possible to the original venue in which William Shakespeare (1564–1616) was a shareholder and actor.

Pass Bear Gardens, which recalls a bear-baiting past, to reach Southwark Bridge, which we cross by going up the steps. But first, it is worth looking in the pedestrian tunnel beneath the bridge to see the evocative engraving that recalls the frost fairs that were held on the tidal Thames. The building of the medieval London Bridge slowed down the river's flow

Opposite: Three centuries of engineering and architecture are represented by Westminster Bridge (1862), the former County Hall Buildings (1908–22) and the London Eye (2000).

because of its narrow arches. The slowness of the river meant that in severe winters the Thames froze over completely, and in 1564 the first frost fair was held, complete with roasting oxen and entertainments. The fairs came to an end in 1814 when a new London Bridge, the next road bridge downstream, was built with broader spans to allow a stronger tide flow. A toll bridge was opened at Southwark in 1819, but people preferred to go downstream to cross at toll-free London Bridge. The bridge here today opened in 1921, true to the style of John Rennie the Elder's original cast-iron structure. After crossing Southwark Bridge, turn left down steps by Vintner's Court to Three Barrels Walk.

Queenhithe and the Fleet

Pass beneath imposing columns fronting Vintner's Court and turn right at the cobbled path bordering the big inlet of Queenhithe for a brief section along the road. Shipwrights during Saxon times operated around the inlet of Queenhithe, until the low medieval London Bridge, built in AD 1000, forced them to move downsteam of it; only shallow-hulled vessels could now berth upstream of the bridge. Together with Billingsgate (see pages 100–110, *Wharves and Warehouses* walk), this was the site of one of London's oldest docks. Some say Queenhithe is named after Matilda, the queen of Henry I (1068–1135); others say that it is derived from the place's early use as a landing place for corn – from the word 'quern', meaning a corn-grinding mill. As you can glean from the local street names, the dock later handled wine. During the 1666 Great Fire of London, Queenhithe was a ferry crossing point for fleeing citizens; many of their valuables, which fell into the river at the time, have since been recovered. In fact, digging along any part of the Thames shore, either here or between the Tower of London and the Houses of Parliament, is now prohibited unless you are a member of the Society of Mudlarks, an association that works in conjunction with the Museum of London.

Turn left at the road, past Stew Lane, along High Timber Street until the signposted left turn back to the Thames Path at Broken Wharf. From here, the route is straightforward, as the Thames Path has opened this stretch to pedestrians. You pass under the Millennium Bridge opposite the Tate Modern on Bankside, where there is a polar sundial presented by London's tylers and bricklayers to mark the millennium and a row of seats backed by trellised arches, and follow the path to the Blackfriars bridges. The northernmost arch of the road bridge is the closest you will get to the Fleet, London's most famous 'lost' river, which was mostly channelled into underground pipes and channels in the mid-18th century. The Anglo-Saxon word 'fleet' referred to a navigable river, but that was long ago; a

Roman barge with a cargo of stone was found buried in the mud near the mouth of the river in 1962 and is now in the Museum of London.

Ancient History
You are now leaving the outer limits of the Roman port of Londinium – which was delineated by the 600-foot (180-m) mouth of the Fleet River and the city wall that reached the Thames at Ludgate – approaching the Saxon port of Lundenwic. The Anglo-Saxons, whose tribes had overrun post-Roman Britain, began their new port in AD 600, on land that stretched between what now lies below Covent Garden and the Strand. At that time, the river spread to where the Strand (meaning beach) runs today and was rich with eels, salmon, roach, pike, mussels and oysters. There were no quays or warehouses; business was done boat-to-shore – the Anglo-Saxon word 'wic', as in Lundenwic, meant market. Goods from settlements throughout Northern Europe were unloaded from Saxon ships, which took on woven cloth for their return journey.

As prosperity increased in the 7th and 8th centuries, Lundenwic attracted the attention of land-hungry Vikings, who attacked during the 9th century. The new timber London Bridge, which the Saxons built in AD 1000, limited passage upstream to those vessels that could pass beneath it at low tide and was as much a defence against Viking invaders as a means of crossing the river. Alfred the Great (849–99) drove out the Vikings in 886, but 100 years later they were back. In some ways the Viking impact on Britain was beneficial, as they were intrepid explorers who had sailed deep into Europe and crossed the Atlantic to North America. They did much to boost London's trade and introduced new cargoes.

Shortly after Blackfriars Bridge, head up the ramp and steps to walk along the riverside road. The elegant Gothic red-brick building on the right after the Art Deco Unilever Building is Sion Hall, which houses an ecclesiastical library; the building dates from 1886. On the river opposite is HMS *President*, a First World War escort ship. HQS *Wellington* served in the Second World War, but is now used as a livery hall for the Company of Master Mariners. The area of gardens and buildings on the right is Temple: the Knights Templar, founded to guard the Church of the Holy Sepulchre in Jerusalem, were based here. The order was supressed by the Pope in 1312 and lawyers moved in. Temple is now one of London's Inns of Court, so-called because in medieval times the buildings were hostelries for barristers and students.

A line of trees at Inner and Middle Temple marks the point where the Great Fire reached in 1666. At the corner of Temple Place, just after Temple Underground Station, is a statue of the great Victorian engineer

Isambard Kingdom Brunel. We are now leaving the City of London, its western limit marked by its armorial dragons on either side of the road.

Bazalgette Strikes Again

The Palladian-style 800-foot (243-m) terrace of Somerset House up on the right is the result of an 18th-century uplift, but the building takes its name from Lord Protector Somerset, who built a house on the site in 1547. The arched recesses in its basement were once watergates, which controlled the flow of water at high tide.

Beyond Waterloo Bridge, the stretch lying ahead of you is Sir Joseph Bazalgette's Victoria Embankment: there's a memorial to him at the far end, just after Charing Cross and Hungerford bridges. Enjoy the decorative cast-iron work: the dolphins on the lamp posts and the benches whose arm-rest motif has changed from camels, within the City of London precincts, to sphinxes, here. Balzalgette's embankment wall was built 14 feet (4.3m) below low-water mark and 20 feet (6m) above high-water mark; laid-out gardens and courtyards were created above the course of the underground. In the 17th and 18th centuries, elegant aristocratic residences, interspersed with coal and timber wharves, lined the shore and the river lapped against the Duke of Buckingham's gardens at York House. The York Watergate, in Victoria Embankment Gardens, led from the duke's garden to the river stairs.

But first you pass, rising above the gardens on the right, the late 19th-century Savoy Hotel, commissioned by Richard D'Oyly Carte (1844–1901), manager of the Gilbert and Sullivan 'Savoy' operettas. The Savoy's cream terracotta tiles where made at the Doulton factory which then sat across the river in Lambeth. On the left is Cleopatra's Needle, an Egyptian obelisk which dates back to *c.* 1475 BC. It has no known historical connection with Cleopatra, who it in fact predates by about 1,400 years. The obelisk was encased in a specially constructed cylindrical pontoon to tow it from Africa, and, after being accidentally dropped in and retrieved from the Bay of Biscay, eventually arrived in England in 1878.

Continue past Embankment Station and the Joseph Balzalgette memorial. Across the road is a bust of Samuel Plimsoll (1824–98) erected by the Seamen's Union 'for his [Plimsoll's] services to men of the sea of all nations'. Plimsoll was responsible for making ships much safer for those who sailed in them, not least by his invention of the Plimsoll line, which indicated safe cargo levels. After the floating hostelry the *Hispaniola*, a former Scottish passenger ship, and the RAF memorial with its inspiring golden eagle, continue to Westminster Bridge and turn right to the underground station.

SPORTING THAMES: PUTNEY–CHISWICK– BARNES–PUTNEY

Summary: We take a break from the hard-working Thames and escape to Putney and beyond, following in the footsteps of Charles II (1630–85) and Nell Gwynn (1650–87), of Victorian Londoners on day trips by train and of wealthy merchants from the port of London looking for out-of-town riverside properties. This is the recreational Thames, for messing about on or beside; a river that is uncluttered by too many bridges, traffic or industry. We dip into rowing and yachting, follow part of the University Boat Race course and experience the impact of the sea on this section of upper tideway. The walk can easily be split into two at Barnes or, if you want a full day out, aim for a pub lunch at Chiswick and digest it on the return journey.

Start and Finish: Putney Bridge Underground Station
Distance: 7 miles (11.7km)
Refreshments: Putney High Street and riverside; Chiswick waterfront; Hammersmith riverfront pubs; Barnes waterfront and village.

The Impact of the Railways

From Putney Bridge Station, turn left and cross the road (Ranelagh Gardens) to a path alongside the railway bridge (signed Thames Path) and turn right at the river. In the 1930s, the railways introduced day excursions at a price that ordinary people could afford. The riverside villages and farmland just outside London became accessible and many boatyards operating pleasure boats opened upstream from Westminster to serve the new customers. It wasn't until the 1880s that the railway reached Putney and, though we cannot see it today, a footpath led from the station platform to a new pier where pleasure steamers awaited.

Follow the path to the right over Swan Drawdock, with its wild water garden at the far (inland) end. Boats drew into the dock at high water and unloaded cargo onto carts on the shore at low tide. Continue along the river to a willow tree and turn right across a paved area, then left to go

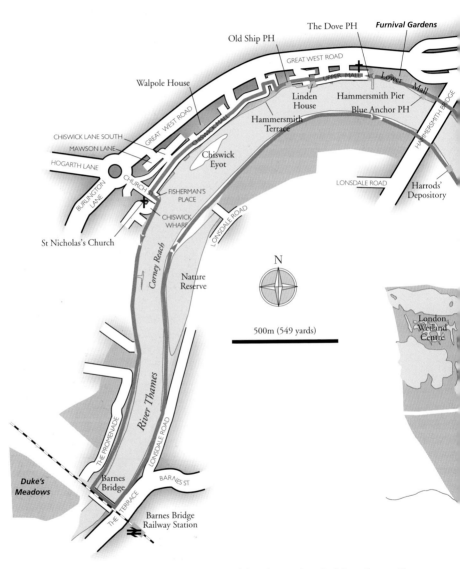

through the foot tunnel beneath the road bridge. This bridge dates from 1884, but its wooden predecessor of 1729 was the first to cross the Thames between London Bridge and Kingston. Putney enjoyed its exclusive crossing point for another 20 years, before Westminster (1750), Blackfriars (1769) and Battersea (1773) bridges were built downstream. Putney Bridge became a watershed between the working and leisure-oriented Thames.

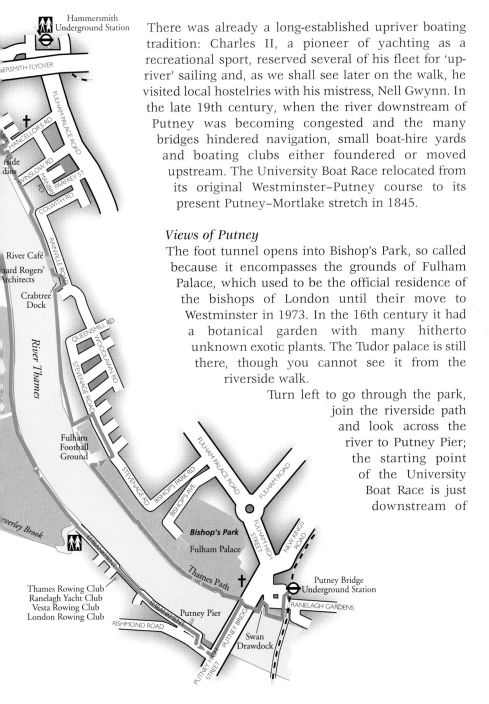

There was already a long-established upriver boating tradition: Charles II, a pioneer of yachting as a recreational sport, reserved several of his fleet for 'up-river' sailing and, as we shall see later on the walk, he visited local hostelries with his mistress, Nell Gwynn. In the late 19th century, when the river downstream of Putney was becoming congested and the many bridges hindered navigation, small boat-hire yards and boating clubs either foundered or moved upstream. The University Boat Race relocated from its original Westminster–Putney course to its present Putney–Mortlake stretch in 1845.

Views of Putney

The foot tunnel opens into Bishop's Park, so called because it encompasses the grounds of Fulham Palace, which used to be the official residence of the bishops of London until their move to Westminster in 1973. In the 16th century it had a botanical garden with many hitherto unknown exotic plants. The Tudor palace is still there, though you cannot see it from the riverside walk.

Turn left to go through the park, join the riverside path and look across the river to Putney Pier; the starting point of the University Boat Race is just downstream of it. The path is an excellent and popular vantage point for the start of the race, which is held in March. A little further along, as you pass beneath the mottled branches of mature London plane trees, look across to see a line of rowing-club boathouses, which you will pass at the end of the walk.

Continue along the path until you have no option but to turn right at the boundary of Fulham Football Ground, leave the park and turn left along Stevenage Road. At the end of the red-brick façade, turn sharp left along a narrow path bordered by a small park and rejoin the river. After you have passed a tiered apartment block, opposite a terrace of yellow-brick houses with tiny gardens, look across the river to where a small obelisk commands an opening in the bankside vegetation. This, which we will look at more closely on the return journey, marks the first mile of the Boat Race's 4 miles and 374 yards (7km).

Richard Rogers' Territory

Our upstream route turns north, as the river's course heads determinedly south, along the downstream side of an enormous meander. The path is punctuated by grassy patches, which provide exhibition space for the occasional rusting sculptures made from machine parts, and the river bank is almost obscured in summer by buddleia. By now, the sultry green folly of Hammersmith Bridge can be seen in the distance, but we are about to leave the riverside for a spell. The path narrows; go up a flight of steps to look along a stretch of river that was once crowded with wharves where market-garden produce was loaded onto barges and taken to feed the London population. The path heads inland and we pass to the right of the Crab Tree pub, which is on the site of the former Crabtree Dock boatyard. Turn left to go past the pub and left again beyond the 1907 Palace Wharf warehouse to return to the riverside path. A modern building of blue, green and glass with an arched roof is the base of Richard Rogers' architectural practice. Peer inside, round the corner where the path opens up into a courtyard area, to see architects' models of building complexes. Rogers is one of the proprietors of the River Café, which is the next building on the right. Look across the river here to where the bulk of Harrods' Depository dominates this stretch of river. The furniture storage house was built in 1894 on the site of market gardens that grew produce for the London markets. Its design echoes that of its parent store in Knightsbridge, central London.

Continue along the path until it heads inland for a fraction, back to the

Opposite: Although much of this route is very popular with walkers, it has a peaceful atmosphere. The broad reach of the Thames here creates an excellent sailing environment, hence the numerous rowing and sailing clubs found here.

river again, then once again inland to circuit Riverside Studios, founded as a film studio by the British actor Jack Buchanan (1891–1957). Pass in front of the studios and take the second left to rejoin the river path at a slipway; you are now on the approach to Hammersmith Bridge.

Bazalgette's Bridge

Hammersmith Bridge is an important landmark for those watching the University Boat Race on television – as it is for the coxes – but it is closed to pedestrians during the race. This was not always the case: in 1870 there were more than 11,000 spectators on the bridge, causing great concern as the structure was already deemed too weak for its weight of road traffic. The great Victorian engineer Sir Joseph Bazalgette designed the present bridge, which opened in 1887. He made the most of the decorative potential of cast iron, then a relatively new building material, making latticework railings, towers topped with French château-style roofs and armorial decorative features. The original bridge, which opened in 1827, was less elaborate but was the first suspension bridge across the Thames. Local resident William Tierney Clarke was the engineer; there's an image of his design on his tomb in the parish church, and it's the subject of engravings found in many a local pub.

Beyond Hammersmith Bridge, round the peak of the loop in the river and then head south along Lower Mall, which is graced by elegant 18th-century houses. If your timing is right, this is a good spot to stop for lunch, for there are a couple of pubs, including the Blue Anchor, which first opened in 1720, and the Dove, a little way further on. Pass Furnival Gardens and Hammersmith Pier with its cluster of barges and houseboats; this is the site of a creek around which the village of Hammersmith grew up. As the name 'Hammersmith' suggests, there was a tradition of iron foundries and forges here, but there were also, in Victorian times, two big breweries, market gardens and brick fields. Furnival Gardens were named after a Victorian philanthropist and scholar who founded a local sculling club. At the end of the gardens, turn right and then immediately left down a flagstoned alley by the 17th-century Dove pub. Just before the pub is the home of the Doves Press and bookbindery, founded jointly by late Victorian style guru William Morris, Thomas Cobden-Sanderson (the man who coined the 'arts and crafts' description of Morris's style revolution) and local print expert Sir Emery Walker. The pub is featured as 'The Pigeons' in a novel called *The Water Gipsies* by politician and humorist A.P. Herbert (1890–1971), who also lived nearby. Charles II and his mistress Nell Gwynn cavorted there and the poet James Thomson (1700–1748) wrote the words of the rousing *Rule Britannia* in a room upstairs.

Illustrious Residents

The tall, red-brick house with five window bays on the right as you return to the riverside path, was the home of William Morris (see pages 111–117, *The Working Wandle* walk) and is where he died. At the end of this stretch of Upper Mall, Linden House – headquarters of the London Corinthian Sailing Club – is set back from the riverside. The crow's-nest structure on a post opposite is the starting box for club races. This broad reach of the river, open to the prevailing south-westerly winds, is considered to be one of the best for sailing on the tidal Thames. Just on the right, after walking beneath the balconies of some apartments, is the Old Ship pub, which dates from the 16th century but was largely rebuilt in the early 19th century. Then there's another patch of public garden, spliced by a white-arcaded wall, which is all that remains of the West Middlesex Water Company pumping station which used to occupy this land. Turn inland here, with the Black Lion pub ahead, and left into Hammersmith Terrace, home of many an illustrious resident, including Sir Emery Walker (1851–1933) and calligrapher Edward Johnston (1872–1944), designer of a celebrated typeface for London Transport.

Soon you are back on the riverside path again at Chiswick Mall, where the 17th- and 18th-century houses are separated from their riverfront gardens by the road. Famous former residents include Barbara Villiers, Countess of Castlemaine, another favourite mistress of Charles II, who lived in Walpole House (dating from between the 16th and 18th centuries). Opposite, at the same level as the road, is Chiswick Eyot, an island with a crop of pollarded willows. You become aware of the encroaching river at high tide: sometimes the next section of the walk is under a foot or so of water, and you may have to make a detour by turning right down Chiswick Lane South, then left and left again to rejoin the path by St Nicholas's Church. Many of the houses have flood defences, such as heavy iron gates or fences backed with plastic casing, a graphic reminder that we are still – downstream of Teddington Lock – subject to the force of the tidal Thames. Twice a day the sea's tides push the river back towards its source and swell its volume; if the river appears to be flowing in the direction in which we are walking – upstream – the tide is 'making', or coming in. Embankments (see pages 149–158, *Bridging the Thames* walk) built downstream aggravated flooding upstream by narrowing the river and increasing its depth: the Thames at Putney is now 9 feet (3m) deeper than it was 300 years ago.

Boat Race Tactics

Here at Corney Reach we are about 3 miles (5km) into the Boat Race course, and racing crews vie for dominance at the part of the stream where the tide flows strongest. As the loop straightens out, the river is exposed to the full force of the prevailing southwesterly winds and if there's a 'wind-over-tide' situation – with the tide going one way and the wind the other – the resulting waves can sink a shallow racing craft. The 'shape', volume and flow of the water change dramatically between high and low tide and the force of the tide is enormous. A wise cox will spend some time talking to local watermen to check the mood of the river, for the course he or she will steer to take advantage of tidal flow is a vital element in racing.

At the end of Chiswick Mall, where the church of St Nicholas, patron saint of sailors, is on the right, turn left to return to the riverside path. The church is the burial place of Barbara Villiers, mistress of Charles II, and of artists William Hogarth (1697–1764) and James McNeill Whistler (1834–1903). Continue past residential developments at Corney Reach until the formal path ends abruptly and enters a field. Triangular ceramic sculptures mark the beginning of Duke's Meadows and you can choose from two or three levels of path, initially bordered by poplars. Continue past an abandoned pavilion, a slipway and a boathouse (from which there are good views over to Barnes riverside) to steps leading up to Barnes Bridge, which you cross.

The three-arched, cast-iron railway bridge was opened in 1849 and, although the footbridge attachment was made especially strong to support Boat Race crowds, it is actually closed for the race. If you are watching from the bank, you cannot see the finish, which is a short way beyond the next

Shoveler

bridge (Chiswick). However, the winner is usually (though by no means always) decided by this point. The crews race against the stream but with the incoming tidal flow, which is about one hour before high water at Putney.

An Oarsman's Paradise

After descending the railway-bridge steps, cross the road and turn right along the footpath beside the road, before veering left down the gravel path to the riverside. Now you can relax from history and architecture, with maybe just the occasional recap as you glimpse places you have passed on the other side of the river, and enjoy a pleasant stroll through a tunnel of trees occasionally interrupted by riverside homes. Inland is the award-winning London Wetland Centre; it is not accessible from the river, but worth a visit to see protected wetland species from all over the world.

You will know when you are a mile or so from Putney Bridge, because you pass the memorial to oarsman and rowing coach Steve Fairbairn, who founded another classic rowing event – the Head of the River Race. There's a footbridge across one of suburban London's surviving rivers, the Beverley Brook, whose course can be followed intermittently to Wimbledon Common and Richmond Park.

The path opens up to a waterfront road flanked by boat clubs: Thames Rowing Club is recognized as one of the world's leading rowing clubs for women, who make up 60 per cent of the membership, and was founded in 1860. Ranelagh Yacht Club, also founded in the mid-19th century, took its name from an 18th-century sailing race from Westminster to Putney Bridge; both the club and the race were forced to move upstream to their present location by 19th-century bridge-building. Vesta is the third oldest rowing club on this stretch, after London and Thames, and is, they say, named after the first tug that sailed past after the club's foundation (the tug, in turn, was named after music-hall star Vesta Tilley). The oldest rowing club is the last we pass: London Rowing Club (LRC) was founded in 1856, although the present balconied clubhouse dates from 1870. Former LRC member and celebrated racing driver Graham Hill and his son Damon wore the dark blue and white club colours on their racing helmets. Traditionally, the LRC was a men-only club, but the first female rowing members were accepted in 2002.

At Boat Race time you may wish to do this walk in reverse in order to catch some of the race. But, unless you can maintain a 15mph (20kmph) sprint to keep up with the crews, you'd better set off early in order to reach a vantage point near the finish at Barnes Bridge or just beyond. To return to Putney Bridge Underground Station, follow the road to the bridge and turn left to cross it.

THAMES-SIDE RETREATS: KEW–RICHMOND

Summary: This walk celebrates the elegant homes and gardens that the Thames-side position has inspired between Kew and Richmond. The upper tidal Thames leaves industry in its place, downstream. Royal palaces were built along this route from medieval times, particularly from the Tudor period. The royals brought with them the most fashionable artists and architects to embellish their country retreats and in their wake came wealthy retainers and merchants enriched by Port of London trade.

Start:	Kew Bridge Railway Station or Kew Gardens Underground and Railway Station
Finish:	Richmond Underground and Railway Station
Distance:	6 miles (10km)
Refreshments:	Kew Gardens Station area; Kew Green; Richmond riverside

If you are starting from Kew Bridge Railway Station, turn right and at the traffic lights cross to Kew Bridge and join the riverside path to go upstream (right) towards Richmond – a 10-minute walk at the most. Alternatively, it takes about 15 minutes to reach the river from Kew Gardens Underground and Railway Station: cross the area in front of the station obliquely right to head down Station Approach. Turn right at the end down Leyborne Park (the alley which runs parallel is rather dark and grubby). Turn left at busy Mortlake Road and, at the traffic lights, cross Kew Road to Kew Green. Cross the Green on the path that goes obliquely behind St Anne's Church, which was built with the help of a £100 donation from Queen Anne in the early 18th century. The slab of gravestone surrounded by railings on the south side of the church is where the 18th-century court painter Thomas Gainsborough (1727–88) is buried.

The elegant Georgian houses round the Green date mainly from the late 18th century, built for courtiers and officials who served King George III's (1738–1820) summer residence at Kew. There have been royal palaces in Kew and Richmond since medieval times, and the Royal Botanic Gardens

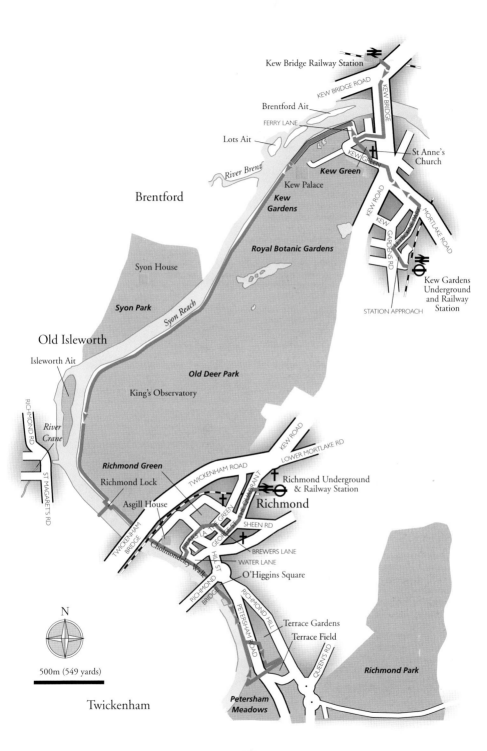

Kew Bridge Railway Station

KEW BRIDGE ROAD

Brentford Ait

FERRY LANE

Lots Ait

KEW BRIDGE

St Anne's Church

KEW GREEN

Kew Green

River Brent

Kew Palace

Kew Gardens

Brentford

KEW ROAD

Royal Botanic Gardens

MORTLAKE ROAD

KEW GARDENS RD

Syon House

Syon Park

Syon Reach

Kew Gardens Underground and Railway Station

STATION APPROACH

Old Isleworth

Isleworth Ait

Old Deer Park

King's Observatory

RICHMOND RD

ST MAGARET'S RD

River Crane

KEW ROAD

LOWER MORTLAKE RD

Richmond Green

Richmond Lock

TWICKENHAM ROAD

THE QUADRANT

Richmond Underground & Railway Station

Asgill House

Richmond

THE GREEN

GEORGE ST

KING ST

PARAY LA.

SHEEN RD

TWICKENHAM BRIDGE

Cholmondeley Walk

HILL ST

BREWERS LANE

WATER LANE

O'Higgins Square

RICHMOND BRIDGE

PETERSHAM ROAD

RICHMOND HILL

Terrace Gardens

Terrace Field

QUEEN'S RD

Richmond Park

N

500m (549 yards)

Petersham Meadows

Twickenham

169

evolved from the gardens that were laid out around the palaces; the main entrance to Kew Gardens is to the left of the Green.

The Making of Kew

The future Queen Caroline, wife of George II (1683–1760), set the ball rolling by hiring William Kent (*c.* 1685–1748) and Charles Bridgeman (d. 1738) – both pioneers in the golden age of naturalistic landscape gardening – to lay out the grounds of Richmond Lodge in the Old Deer Park, which we pass later. At the time of Caroline's death, in 1737, the gardens reached as far as today's Kew. But it was her son Frederick and his wife Augusta who were responsible for creating the first Kew Gardens around their (since demolished) palace. After Frederick's death, Augusta, with the help of architects and horticulturalists, began collecting rare and exotic plants. Some of the trees planted at that time are still living, including the first pagoda and ginkgo trees introduced to England, and the Orangery and Pagoda (the structure as opposed to the tree) are surviving buildings. The next king, George III, built on Augusta's work and, with the naturalist Sir Joseph Banks (1743–1820), consolidated Kew's place as a superlative collection of plants from around the world, and opened the gardens to the public.

Cross from the Green to Ferry Lane, which once led to the Brentford ferry that carried horses, carriages and people across the river from the mid-17th century until the 20th century. Turn left along the river bank (signed Kew Gardens), via the towpath. Just downstream, the first Kew Bridge was built in the 1750s, though the present bridge dates from 1903.

Across the river is Brentford (see pages 20–26, *A Flight of Locks* walk) and an island called Brentford Ait that is lush in high summer with oak, willow and poplar trees in full leaf. Between the 14th and 18th centuries, osier willows for basket-making were cultivated on the island. The word 'ait' is a corruption of the Anglo-Saxon *eyot* (islet). There are several aits along the river, formed from silts and gravels washed down by tributary rivers. The next is Lots Ait and shortly afterwards you can see where the River Brent meets the Thames.

In the 18th century, the elegance of Brentford almost matched that of Kew and Richmond. In the 19th century, however, the outlet you see across the river was a busy dock, where the Grand Junction (later Grand

Opposite: Look from the towpath over a pond, which in high summer is rich in wildlife and alive with dragonflies, to the grassy expanse of the Old Deer Park, whose obelisk is so positioned that you can look along the meridian line that preceded the one at Greenwich.

Union) Canal joined the Thames, and was later the terminus of a branch line of Isambard Kingdom Brunel's Great Western Railway. Instead of the smart marina and waterside development there today, you would have seen concentrated activity: barges lined up along the wharves, some laden with coal and lime and others ready to take produce from market gardens or hay for the working horses of London. From the mid-19th century until the dock's closure in the 1960s, the scene was packed with warehouses and railway freight yards.

Syon Park and the Old Deer Park

Meanwhile, on the left, you can gain some idea of the extent of Princess Augusta's Kew Gardens as you walk along their western boundary. Individual features are hidden by bank and trees until, towards the end, you look over an area of wild meadow planting. The vista over the river opens up at Syon Park, our next palatial Thames-side residence. This one has been the home of the Percy family, earls of Northumberland, since 1594. The lion above the clock tower was transported by barge along the Thames from a Northumberland family home in the Strand. The name is taken from Sion Hill in Palestine and the house, of which the original Tudor shell remains, was built on the site of a medieval convent. In the second half of the 18th century, the house and grounds had a complete makeover by another couple of style giants of the period: architect-designer Robert Adam (1728–92) and landcsape gardener Lancelot 'Capability' Brown (1715–83). The tidal meadow, so called because the river floods over it twice daily at high tide – a rarity for the crowded banks of the Thames – has been designated a Site of Special Scientific Interest.

The whole of the Thames along this stretch is an inviting corridor for wildlife, with freshwater habitats now taking over from the salt-marsh that dominates further downstream. The sea tide reaches as far as Teddington Lock further upstream, but its salty influence is more diluted here. Soon you'll see a pink and white confection of a building on the riverside, which is the very splendid Pavilion built to the design of Robert Mylne in 1803. It originally adjoined the boathouse where the Duke of Northumberland's state barge, which was probably used for entertaining, was kept.

The path is now raised above the main river and an overflow channel. Excavated earth built up the path, which doubled as a dyke against river flood water. The way runs through a tunnel of trees alongside Syon Reach; keep your eyes on the alert above for some splendid specimens of beefsteak fungus. Soon, about an hour into the walk, there's a break in the trees, overlooking a pond rich in flowers and hunted by red darter dragonflies in summer, and a view that opens out across the Old Deer

Park, royal hunting grounds of 700 years ago. This is where Richmond Lodge was sited, official residence of the future King George II and Queen Caroline when Caroline started her gardening plans. Look between the twin steel obelisks along the meridian line by which the king's time was set before Greenwich took over this role in 1884. The Observatory itself was commissioned by George III, who wanted the best chance of watching the transit of the star Venus in 1769. Today, the Old Deer Park is owned by the Crown Estate and is open to the public.

Old Isleworth to Richmond

Now, on the opposite bank, we are passing what could almost pass for a rural English village, but is in fact Old Isleworth. There's a sign advertising the Isleworth ferry, which operates at weekends from May to September. In the 19th century the village was surrounded by market gardens producing strawberries, raspberries and other fruit for London markets. Knowing how the islets of the Thames form, it is no surprise that just upstream of Isleworth Ait is the outlet of the River Crane, from which, in the Middle Ages, a channel was cut to power the corn mill at Syon Abbey. The little hamlet of Twickenham, now a widespread suburban area on the far bank, grew up in the fork of land between the Thames and the Crane.

Continue to Richmond Lock, which was completed in 1894 and the last lock on the downstream course of the Thames. Take a brief detour up to the footbridge to look down at the great chambers and gates. The lock and weir were designed to increase the river's depth and flow to prevent the build-up of silt and sewage; this was becoming such a serious problem in the late 19th century that pleasure boats would run aground and the river was reduced to a noisome trickle. So much water was being extracted to meet the enormous demands of the downstream metropolis, said the engineers, that the river's upstream flow couldn't carry it. Not only did it have to cope with local sewage, but also that which was swept upstream from London on the incoming tide.

A few yards after the lock, you pass beneath the concrete arches and bronze balustrades of Twickenham Bridge (1933) and another bridge that carried the railway to Richmond from 1846. You are now on the outskirts of Richmond. On the left is Asgill House (1758), home of wealthy City banker and one-time mayor of London, Sir Charles Asgill. When Sir Charles threw a party for his City associates, guests were ferried upriver in barges with on-board bands. Pleasure, and even ceremonial, barges must often have added glamour to this stretch of the Thames as the rich and royal made their visits. Prince Frederick (of Kew Gardens fame) was also a great party host of the 18th century, bringing in orchestras, theatricals and masquerades. He loved the river and was a great supporter of rowing races. He commissioned his house architect William Kent to design a state barge, which he used for musical concerts as well as for ferrying his family along the river.

One of the most magnificent and poignant sights, however, must have been that of Queen Elizabeth I on her last voyage from Richmond Palace by barge as the poet William Camden described: 'The Queen was brought by water to Whitehall/At every stroke the oars did tears fall'. Continue along Cholmondeley Walk, with its eminently stylish bow-windowed Georgian residences and, when you cross Water Lane – which you may have to negotiate at high tide – you will have arrived in riverside café land and the broad, stepped terraces beneath a modern Neo-classical-style development.

Into the Heart of Richmond

Continue beside the river, past the boat-building sheds and under Richmond Bridge. The soft grey Purbeck stone lines of the original 1777 structure were cleverly preserved when the bridge had to be widened in 1939. Your distance from London Bridge is now $11\frac{1}{4}$ miles (18.8km) by river, while upstream, 15 river miles away, is Windsor. Immediately after the bridge pass beneath O'Higgins Square, named after General Bernardo O'Higgins (c. 1778–1842), Chilean statesman (of Irish extraction) and liberator of his country from the Spanish, who studied in Richmond for three years from 1795. After five minutes or so, you will pass Richmond canoe clubs on the left just before a large white building, a former pub. Here, strike up through the gardens left away

Beefsteak fungus

from the river and cross Petersham Road into Terrace Gardens. Follow the paths up and right through the gardens, noting the coadestone statue of the River God Thames, which was the single most expensive item in the 'Coadestone Catalogue of Architectural Statuary and Ornament' of 1784.

The reason for this detour away from the river becomes obvious as soon as you emerge from the gardens in the top right-hand corner. Here, from a gravelled terrace on Richmond Hill, high above the river, is a view that has inspired many an artist and writer, including J.M.W. Turner, Charles Dickens, Sir Walter Scott (1771–1832) and Robert Bridges (1844–1930). You can read excerpts from their poems and identify points of view with the help of information panels. The houses above the terrace are highly sought after, while immediately below are the Petersham Meadows where horses and cows still graze.

Cut down a path that goes straight through Terrace Field just beyond the information panels. Cross Petersham Road again and turn right along the riverside path. Head back towards Richmond Bridge, past the expensive Canyon Café (check inside for glimpses of the rich and famous) and the largest plane tree in the capital, under the bridge and across Water Lane. Take Friars Lane, the next turning right, and cross Richmond Green, with its elegant border of Queen Anne and Georgian houses, obliquely right. The Green was once the scene of jousting tournaments. Turn right through Brewers Lane into George Street and head left uphill until you see Richmond Underground and Railway Station on your right.

GAZETTEER

This gazetteer provides contact details and opening times of public places mentioned in the text relevant to docks, rivers or canals in walk order:

Perivale Wood Local Nature Reserve
Perivale, London UB6
www.biochem.ucl.ac.uk
Access for parties by appointment only, unless you are a member of the Selborne Society.

Horsenden Hill Visitor Centre
Horsenden Lane North,
Greenford, London UB6 7PB
Tel: 020 8825 6640

The Canal Museum
12–13 New Wharf Road,
King's Cross, London N1 9RT
Tel: 020 7713 0836
www.canalmuseum.org.uk
Open Tuesday–Sunday, plus Bank Holiday Mondays, 10am–4.30pm.

Camden Lock Market
Camden Lock Place,
Chalk Farm Road,
London NW1 8AF
Tel: 020 7284 2084.
www.camdenlockmarket.com
Open daily, 10am–6pm.

Museum in Docklands
No. 1 Warehouse, West India Quay,
Hertsmere Road, London E14 4AL
Tel: 0870 444 3857
www.museumindocklands.org.uk
Open daily, 10am–6pm.

Island History Trust
The Dockland Settlement,
197 East Ferry Road,
London E14 3BA
Tel: 020 7987 6041
www.islandhistory.org.uk
Open Tuesdays and Wednesdays and the first Sunday of each month, 1.30–4.30pm; visits at other times by appointment only.

Mudchute City Farm
Pier Street, Isle of Dogs,
London E14 3HP
Tel: 020 7515 5901
www.mudchute.org
Open daily, 10am–4pm.

Cutty Sark
King William Walk, Greenwich,
London SE10 9HT
Tel: 020 8858 3445
www.cuttysark.org.uk
Open daily, 10am–5pm.

Royal Naval College
Greenwich, London SE10 9LW
Tel: 020 8269 4747
www.greenwichfoundation.org.uk
Grounds open daily, 8am–6pm;
Painted hall and Chapel open daily, 10am–5pm.

Royal Observatory, National Maritime Museum and Queen's House
Park Row, Greenwich,
London SE10 9JF
Tel: 020 8858 4422
www.nmm.ac.uk
Open daily, 10am–5pm.

Brunel Engine House
Railway Avenue, Rotherhithe,
London SE16 4LF
Tel: 020 7231 3840
www.brunelenginehouse.org.uk
April–October, Saturday and Sunday,
1–5pm; November–March, Sundays,
1–5pm.

*Thames Barrier Information
and Learning Centre*
1 Unity Way, Woolwich,
London SE18 5NJ
Tel: 020 8305 4188
Open daily, October–March,
11am–3.30pm; April–September
10.30am–4.30pm.

*Bramah Museum of
Tea and Coffee*
40 Southwark Street,
London SE1 1UN
Tel: 020 7403 5650
www.bramahmuseum.co.uk
Open daily, 10am–6pm.

City Hall
The Queen's Walk,
London SE1 2AA
Tel: 020 7983 4000
www.london.gov.uk
Open Monday–Friday, 8am–8pm;
check website for open weekends.

Tower Bridge
London SE1 2UP
Tel: 020 7403 3761
www.towerbridge.org.uk
Open daily, 10am–5.30pm
(summer); 9.30am–5pm (winter).

HMS Belfast
Morgan's Lane, Tooley Street,
London SE1 2JH
Tel: 020 7940 6320
www.iwm.org.uk/belfast
Open daily, 10am–6pm (summer) and
10am–5pm (winter).

Golden Hinde
St Mary Overie Dock,
Cathedral Street,
London SE1 9DE
Tel: 08700 118700
www.goldenhinde.co.uk
Open daily, times vary so call in
advance.

Pumphouse Educational Museum
Lavender Pond and Nature Park,
Lavender Road, Rotherhithe,
London SE16 5DZ
Tel: 020 7231 2976
www.se16.btinternet.co.uk/
pumphouse.htm
Open Monday–Friday, 9.30am–3.30pm.

Young's Brewery
Brewery Tap Visitor Centre,
68 High Street, Wandsworth,
London SW18 4LB
Tel: 020 8875 7005
www.youngs.co.uk
Open Monday–Friday, 11am–5.30pm;
Saturday 12 noon–5pm. Tours at 12
noon on Tuesdays, Wednesdays,
Thursdays and Saturdays.

Wandsworth Museum
The Courthouse, 11 Garratt Lane,
Wandsworth, London SW18 4AQ
Tel: 020 8871 7074
www.wandsworth.gov.uk/museum
Open Tuesday–Friday, 10am–5pm;
weekends, 2–5pm.

Merton Abbey Mills
Watermill Way,
London SW19 2RD
Tel: 020 8543 9608
www.mertonabbeymills.com
Shops open daily.

Morden Hall Park
Morden Hall Road,
London SM4 5JD
Tel: 020 8545 6850
www.nationaltrust.org.uk
Open daily, 8am–6pm.

Lee Valley Park Information Centre
Lee Valley Park Farm, Stubbins Hall
Lane, Crooked Mile, Waltham Abbey,
Essex EN9 2EG
Tel: 01992 702200
www.leevalleypark.org.uk
Open Monday–Friday 10am–4pm;
weekends 10am–5pm.

**Middlesex Filter Beds
Nature Reserve**
Lea Bridge Road, Leyton,
London E10
Tel: 01992 70220
Open weekends and bank holidays,
10am–6pm (summer); school
summer holidays and summer half-
term, Monday–Friday, 10am–5pm;
weekends and bank holidays,
10am–4pm (winter).

Three Mills
Three Mill Lane,
London E3 3DU
Tel: 020 7363 3336
www.threemills.com
Open Monday–Friday, 8am–6pm.

Museum of Garden History
Lambeth Palace Road,
London SE1 7LB
Tel: 020 7401 8865
Open daily 10.30am–5pm.

London Wetland Centre
Queen Elizabeth's Walk, Barnes,
London SW13 9WT
Tel: 020 8409 4400
www.wwt.org.uk
Open daily, 9.30am–6pm (summer, last
admission 5pm), 9.30am–5pm (winter,
last admission 4pm).

Kew Bridge Steam Museum
Green Dragon Lane,
Brentford, Middlesex TW8 0EN
Tel: 020 8568 4757
www.kbsm.org
Open daily, 11am–5pm; the engines
are in steam on weekends and bank
holidays.

Royal Botanic Gardens
Kew, Richmond,
Surrey TW9 3AB
Tel: 020 8332 5655
www.rbgkew.org.uk
Open weekdays, 9.30am–6.30pm,
weekends and bank holidays
9.30am–7.30pm (summer);
9.30am–6pm (September–October);
9.30am–4.15pm (winter).

BIBLIOGRAPHY

Pevsner Architectural Guides to London Nikolaus Pevsner (various dates)

London Docklands, An Architectural Guide Elizabeth Williamson & Nikolaus Pevsner (Penguin Books, 1998)

The Times *London History Atlas* ed. H. Clout (Times Books, 1991)

Geology of London and South-east England G.M. Davies (1939)

The Lost Rivers of London Nicholas Barton (Historical Publications, 1992)

London, Biography of a City Christopher Hibbert (Penguin Books, 1980)

Dockland S.K. Al Naib (Thames and Hudson, 1986)

Canals and Waterways Michael E. Ware (Shire Publications Ltd, 1995)

A Guide to London's Riverside Suzanne Ebel and Doreen Impey (Constable, 1985)

London, A Biography Peter Ackroyd (Vintage, 2001)

London and Docklands Walks S.K. Al Naib (University of East London, 2000)

The Green London Way Bob Gilbert (Lawrence & Wishart, 1991)

Time Out *Book of London Walks* ed. Andrew White (Penguin Books, 2001)

Canal Walks: South Ray Quinlan (Sutton Publishing, 1994)

Walks Along the Thames Path Ron Emmons (New Holland, 2001)

Andrew Duncan's Favourite London Walks Andrew Duncan (New Holland, 2002)

Wandsworth Past Dorian Gerhold (Historical Publications, 1998)

Wren's London Eric de Maré (Michael Joseph, 1977)

The National Trust Guide to Our Industrial Past Anthony Burton (Mitchell Beazley, 1983)

INDEX

WEBSITES

www.bb-environment.org
www.brent.gov.uk
www.brentford-dock.net
www.britainexpress.com
www.britishwaterways.co.uk
www.brunelenginehouse.org.uk
www.canalsguide.co.uk
www.environment-agency.gov.uk
www.fls.org.jm
www.greenwich-guide.org.uk

www.historychannel.com
www.islandhistory.org.uk
www.lddc-history.org.uk
www.southwark,gov.uk
www.thames.org.uk
www.the-river-thames.co.uk
www.thhol.freeserve.co.uk
www.touruk.co.uk/london
www.towerhamlets.gov.uk
www.victorianlondon.org

ACKNOWLEDGEMENTS

With special thanks to Chris Elmers at Museum in Docklands, the Canal Museum for help in research, Nick Fordham for checking some of the routes, and my husband Robin for running Walking Plus while I was writing.

Photographs:
Front cover, pages 2, 49, 75, 155: LondonStills.com
Page 79: Chris Coe